THE NEW ECUMENISM

THE NEW ECUMENISM

HOW THE CATHOLIC CHURCH AFTER VATICAN II TOOK OVER
THE LEADERSHIP OF THE WORLD ECUMENICAL MOVEMENT

KENNETH D. WHITEHEAD

ST PAULS

Library of Congress Cataloging-in-Publication Data

Whitehead, Kenneth D.
  The new ecumenism: how the Catholic Church after Vatican II took over the
leadership of the world ecumenical movement / by Kenneth D. Whitehead.
      p. cm.
  Includes bibliographical references.
  ISBN 978-0-8189-1283-2
  1. Ecumenical movement—History—20th century. 2. Catholic Church—Relations.
I. Title.
  BX6.5.W45   2009
  280'.042—dc22

                              2008032775

Produced and designed in the United States of America by the
Fathers and Brothers of the Society of St. Paul,
2187 Victory Boulevard, Staten Island, New York 10314-6603
as part of their communications apostolate.

ISBN 10: 0-8189-1283-9
ISBN 13: 978-0-8189-1283-2

Printing Information:

Current Printing - first digit   1   2   3   4   5   6   7   8   9   10

Year of Current Printing - first year shown

2009   2010   2011   2012   2013   2014   2015   2016   2017   2018

Nourished and sustained by the Eucharist, Catholics cannot but feel encouraged to strive for the full unity for which Christ expressed so ardent a hope in the Upper Room. The Successor of Peter knows that he must make himself especially responsible for his Divine Master's supreme aspiration. Indeed, he is entrusted with the task of strengthening his brethren (cf. Lk 22:32). With full awareness, therefore, at the beginning of his ministry in the Church of Rome that Peter bathed in his blood, Peter's current Successor takes on *as his primary task* the duty to work tirelessly to rebuild the full and visible unity of all Christ's followers (emphasis added).

First Message of His Holiness Pope Benedict XVI
at the end of the Eucharistic Concelebration with
Members of the College of Cardinals in the
Sistine Chapel, Wednesday, April 20, 2005

To
Jude Daurelle

TABLE OF CONTENTS

Biblical Abbreviations

OLD TESTAMENT

Genesis	Gn	Nehemiah	Ne	Baruch	Ba
Exodus	Ex	Tobit	Tb	Ezekiel	Ezk
Leviticus	Lv	Judith	Jdt	Daniel	Dn
Numbers	Nb	Esther	Est	Hosea	Ho
Deuteronomy	Dt	1 Maccabees	1 M	Joel	Jl
Joshua	Jos	2 Maccabees	2 M	Amos	Am
Judges	Jg	Job	Jb	Obadiah	Ob
Ruth	Rt	Psalms	Ps	Jonah	Jon
1 Samuel	1 S	Proverbs	Pr	Micah	Mi
2 Samuel	2 S	Ecclesiastes	Ec	Nahum	Na
1 Kings	1 K	Song of Songs	Sg	Habakkuk	Hab
2 Kings	2 K	Wisdom	Ws	Zephaniah	Zp
1 Chronicles	1 Ch	Sirach	Si	Haggai	Hg
2 Chronicles	2 Ch	Isaiah	Is	Malachi	Ml
Ezra	Ezr	Jeremiah	Jr	Zechariah	Zc
		Lamentations	Lm		

NEW TESTAMENT

Matthew	Mt	Ephesians	Eph	Hebrews	Heb
Mark	Mk	Philippians	Ph	James	Jm
Luke	Lk	Colossians	Col	1 Peter	1 P
John	Jn	1 Thessalonians	1 Th	2 Peter	2 P
Acts	Ac	2 Thessalonians	2 Th	1 John	1 Jn
Romans	Rm	1 Timothy	1 Tm	2 John	2 Jn
1 Corinthians	1 Cor	2 Timothy	2 Tm	3 John	3 Jn
2 Corinthians	2 Cor	Titus	Tt	Jude	Jude
Galatians	Gal	Philemon	Phm	Revelation	Rv

CHAPTER ONE

THE CATHOLIC CHURCH'S NEW
ECUMENICAL VENTURE

I pray... for those who believe in me... that they may
all be one; even as thou, Father, art in me and I in thee,
that they may also be in us, that the world may believe
that thou hast sent me.   *John 17:20-21*

THIS PRAYER OF Christ's was no doubt heartfelt. Surely Our
Lord meant what he said when he prayed "that they may
all be one." For him the unity of Christians was one of the
things that would help bring the world to believe that he was the
Savior of that same world. Nevertheless, many of those who profess
themselves to be followers of Christ today do not seem to think it
is very important whether or not they really agree with, or take any
specific actions to be in agreement with, their fellow Christians on
basic Christian beliefs. Christ's prayer has regularly fallen on many
deaf ears. Christians have too often actually been at odds with each
other, in fact. Christianity is a divided religion, and has been for
centuries. Christians are *not* "one," unfortunately, as Christ prayed
they would be.

Since the end of the Second Vatican Council some forty-plus
years ago, the Catholic Church has been engaged in a renewed effort to seek reunion with other Christians in response to this prayer

of Christ. The Church has produced and carefully put forward several key documents on the subject of a renewed quest for Christian unity, and she is also regularly and steadily involved pretty much at all levels today in taking practical steps to try to achieve it. The last several popes, in particular, have made this quest an item of the highest priority on their agendas. This has been true to perhaps a much greater extent than most Catholics have generally noticed or realized. Yet it is hard to imagine on what John Paul II, for example, put in more time and effort, personally, than he did on his efforts to seek better relations with our fellow Christians. And from the time of his election to the chair of Peter in 2005, Benedict XVI has followed pretty much the same pattern.

These popes have been acting in this area in response to a mandate of the Second Vatican Council. That often misunderstood Council truly did inaugurate a whole new era in "ecumenism" for the Catholic Church. By "ecumenism" here is meant relationships with other Christians and Christian bodies, and the search for the Christian unity for which Christ prayed. The Council's principal work in this regard is to be found in its Decree on Ecumenism, *Unitatis Redintegratio* ("Restoration of Unity"), promulgated on November 21, 1964, at the end of the Council's Third Session. We shall be devoting major attention to what this document has to say, as well as to the way in which the Church has regularly acted upon it in the years since the Council.

It is true that the term "ecumenism" is sometimes also used to refer to relations not only with non-Catholic Christians, but also with non-Christians. It is also true that the ecumenical impulse is in some ways inseparable from the missionary impulse — the desire to win souls for Christ. Indeed, the Church herself has made clear that these two impulses are related, and in some ways, they are inseparable.

However, the Council issued a separate Decree on the Church's Missionary Activity, *Ad Gentes Divinitus,* on the task of making converts, just as it issued yet another separate Declaration on the

Relation of the Church to Non-Christian Religions, *Nostra Aetate*. Both of these documents were approved in 1965, and deal authoritatively with how Catholics are to treat non-Catholic Christians *and* those who are not Christians at all, but in many cases profess another religion (which they believe to be true).

In this book, we shall not deal with the larger question of the claims and proofs of which world religion is in fact true and why. This book starts rather with the basic premise that the one, holy, Catholic, and apostolic Church — described in the Nicene Creed still professed by Catholics on Sundays and holy days and taught by the popes and the bishops in union with him — *is* the true Church of Christ, and that those who believe in Christ ought therefore to be part of this Church in fulfillment of Christ's prayer.

Millions of Christians who profess to believe in Christ, though, do *not* believe in the Church which Christ himself said he would build on the rock of Peter (cf. Mt 16:18). Even some of the Christians who do believe that Christ did indeed found a Church, which has lasted down to our day and still exists in the world, do not necessarily believe that the Catholic Church headed by the pope and the bishops in union with him, *is* the Church Christ founded. The fifteen or so Eastern Orthodox Churches, for example, believe that *they* constitute the "one, holy, Catholic, and apostolic" Church professed in the Creed.

It is therefore the subject of ecumenism itself, then — the Catholic Church's relations with other Christians, and with the search for Christian unity — that we will be dealing with in this book. How we should deal with non-Christians, those who adhere to another religious faith entirely, or those who do not accept any reality beyond human experience at all, will have to be the subject of another discussion on another occasion.

Agreement is far from universal among Catholics themselves whether the new Catholic emphasis on ecumenism adopted by Vatican Council II has been an entirely good thing for the Church. Among the various misunderstandings and confusions that followed in the wake of the Council, those related to the question of ecumenism have in fact seemed to be especially acute. And this is not just because of the apparent lack of success to date of the really extraordinary ecumenical efforts the Church has made in the post-conciliar years. For after more than forty years of such ecumenical efforts, there is scarcely a single case of completely restored Christian unity; nor, in spite of widely publicized ecumenical meetings between Church leaders, extensive dialogue by theologians, numerous agreed statements, many and regular joint prayers for Christian unity, along with much talk on all sides about how Christians *ought* to be united, there still does not seem, any time soon, to be much of a real prospect for actual Christian reunification, or restoration of communion between formerly separated Christian bodies,

There has, of course, been a great deal of dialogue between the Catholic Church and most other organized Christian Churches or ecclesial communities. Expressions of good will have been frequent, and many areas of agreement have been identified and described. Nevertheless, there has been little real movement towards any actual reunion. Meanwhile, new obstacles to a unity once thought to be closer have arisen, for example, the ordination of women and of active homosexuals in some of the provinces of the Anglican Communion; and thus any possible reunion in such cases as these now actually seems farther away than ever.

At the same time, the Catholic Church's diligent and continuing ecumenical efforts have sometimes met with actual rebuffs, and even with outright rejection, as in the case of some of the dramatic appeals for Christian unity that came from Pope John Paul II, such as those addressed to the Orthodox in Greece, Russia, Georgia, or Mount Sinai, where the welcome accorded to the pope's appeals seemed considerably less than enthusiastic. Similarly, when John Paul II visited Scandinavia, several Lutheran bishops pointedly boycotted him. (We nevertheless have to remember however, that at least the pope was *received* in most of these places!)

Beyond that, another perceived problem with the new Catholic emphasis on ecumenism is the very real temptation to minimize areas of disagreement — such as common Protestant objections to the veneration of the Blessed Virgin Mary — in order to reach agreements. This can be a very real temptation, in fact. Many knowledgeable and committed Catholics believe that the Church's post-Vatican II emphasis on ecumenism has been one of the factors that has weakened Catholic doctrinal orthodoxy, particularly the belief, certainly not changed by Vatican II, that the Catholic Church remains the one, true Church of Christ. The Council's Dogmatic Constitution on the Church, *Lumen Gentium*, in particular, was at pains to emphasize that the Catholic Church alone possesses the fullness of Christ's revealed truth and the fullness of the sacramental means of sanctification and salvation in Christ. This document expressly teaches that "this is the *sole* Church of Christ which in the Creed we profess to be one, holy, Catholic, and apostolic" (LG 8; emphasis added).

Nevertheless, this is not necessarily the dominant *impression* that the Church has generally conveyed to the world in the postconciliar era. Rather, in her contemporary ecumenical outreach, the Catholic Church often gives the impression, at least among those not looking too carefully at the details (which includes most people), that she does *not* insist as strongly on her claims as she used to. Certainly she no longer confronts the world as the exclusive and intransigent body she was once largely seen to be, but rather now strives to present herself as irenic, accommodating, and agreeable.

Moreover, if the Catholic Church indeed teaches Christ's saving truths in their most complete form, and, similarly, offers all the sacramental means introduced into the world by Christ to help in our sanctification and salvation, then for the Church to enter into "dialogue" with other Churches or Christian bodies which, by definition, do *not* possess and offer all these same truths and means of grace in their fullness, the new ecumenical approach almost inevitably appears to some to weaken and even compromise the Church's own teaching and example.

How can the Catholic Church possibly enter into a *debate*

about the truths and means confided to her by Christ and transmitted down to us by means of the apostolic succession of bishops? To enter into such a debate about these things seems to admit that there can be more than one point of view about them. At the very least, this seems to leave open the question of whether the Church is perhaps *not*, after all, everything that she claims to be. It suggests that perhaps she is not totally confident about what human beings must believe and do in order to achieve their salvation and sanctification in Jesus Christ. Others may claim to know of an equally valid road to travel, as, indeed, many do so claim, in their characteristic ways, whether they are Evangelicals, Eastern Orthodox, or others. By entering into dialogue with them, the Church almost inescapably accords them at least a measure of legitimacy.

Such is the logic which has not ceased to prompt questions about how the Catholic Church, considering what she claims to be, could possibly become just another "partner" in the ecumenical "dialogue," just another Christian denomination, as it were. This logic, for a very long time, certainly did govern the Church's own attitude towards ecumenism, and there is no question but that the Church's truth claims *can* be down-played and even compromised by a too-eager plunge into ecumenical dialogue. For example, in explaining why Catholics could not take part in the organized ecumenical movement, which began under Protestant auspices in the early part of the twentieth century, Pope Pius XI, in his encyclical on Religious Unity, *Mortalium Animos*, issued on January 6, 1928, was moved to ask, rhetorically: "Shall we suffer what would indeed be iniquitous, the truth, and truth divinely revealed, to be made a subject for compromise?" (MA 8).

Pope Pius XI saw the ecumenical movement of his day as pursuing the noblest of ideas by promoting charity among all Christians. Nevertheless, he wondered: "How does it happen that this charity tends to injure faith?" In the Catholic view, according to this pontiff, who reigned between the two world wars, "the disciples of Christ must be united principally by the bond of *one faith*" (MA #9;

emphasis added) — namely, the faith taught by the magisterium of the Catholic Church. Pius XI even granted that Christians engaged in the ecumenical movement might even have been motivated by the same prayer of Christ from John 17 that appears at the head of this chapter. Nevertheless, as he saw it, they were attempting to seek unity on the basis of something less than the fullness of Christian truth, and hence, in his view, their efforts were doomed to failure.

Describing Christian ecumenists, however sincere, as "pan-Christians," Pius XI thus saw the ecumenical movement as a "federation" of churches, or an "assembly" of those calling themselves Christians, while not being in agreement even with one another on what constituted Christianity. He concluded, therefore, that "it should be clear why the Apostolic See has never allowed its subjects to take part in the[se] assemblies of non-Catholics: for the union of Christians can only be promoted by promoting the return to the one true Church of Christ of those who are separated from it, for in the past they have unhappily left it" (MA 10).

This was the official stance of the Catholic Church on ecumenism up until Vatican Council II: Christian unity was to be brought about by a "return" of non-Catholic Christians to the Catholic fold. This theme of a return was mentioned in nearly every Church statement or document bearing upon the question of ecumenism. Typical was the following mention by Pope Leo XIII in his 1894 *Praeclara Gratulationis*, when he declared that "the yearning desire of Our heart bids Us conceive the hope that the day is not far distant, when the Eastern Churches, so illustrious in their ancient faith and glorious past, will return to the fold they have abandoned." In fact, the day in question envisaged by Leo apparently *was* "far distant," however, since the Eastern Churches, among others, showed scarcely any disposition whatever to consider any such return — rather the contrary: they still largely consider that it was the Catholic Church that had abandoned communion with *them*.

Nevertheless, the Catholic Church did not cease calling for such a return to her fold anyway. On the eve of Vatican II itself, in his first encyclical *Ad Petri Cathedram,* issued on June 29, 1959, Blessed Pope John XXIII, though he spoke more lovingly of Christians separated from the Catholic Church than perhaps had been the custom, nevertheless passed in review all the reasons why true Christian unity still resided within the Catholic Church; and, on that basis, he addressed himself to all separated Christians by asking: "May we, in fond anticipation, address you as sons and brethren? May we hope with a father's love for your *return*?" (APC 79; emphasis added).

Thus, the idea of a simple "return" continued to be the ecumenical *Leitmotiv* as far as the Catholic Church was concerned. Although the Church prayed for Christian unity, and for many decades devoted a week in January to an Octave of Prayers for such unity — as she does today — these prayers themselves generally implied that what was involved was a simple return to the true Church by the Protestants, along with an end to the schism with the Orthodox.

What the Second Vatican Council did with regard to ecumenism, however — as was the case in so many other areas — was not to change or contradict what these previous popes had decided and taught (which in any case the Council had no power to change); but rather to look at the whole question of ecumenism from a different angle, and try to approach it in a different way — to change the terms of the discussion, as it were. The idea was to try to launch a new start towards Christian unity by stepping around at least some past obstacles and leaving at least some past quarrels behind. There was to be no compromise concerning Catholic truth, including the truth that the Catholic Church was the unique Church founded by Christ. Catholic truth was to be reaffirmed in its entirety. No longer, however, would the Church simply wait around passively for an already long awaited but continually delayed and indeed steadily rejected "return."

For it was pretty clear that, except for a trickle of individual converts, it did not seem at all likely that many or even any non-Catholic Christian Churches or communions were in any way contemplating, or would contemplate, any such return. Nor did most separated Christians generally see themselves as having "left" or "abandoned" or been "separated" from the Catholic Church. Their ancestors certainly did, but living adherents of these non-Catholic Churches and communions had never themselves enjoyed the fullness of the faith as found in the Catholic Church, so she was hardly something they could leave or abandon or separate themselves from. For most of them the idea of a "return" was almost meaningless, in fact; and to the extent that any ecumenical dialogue with them might or did take place, it was almost bound to be a dialogue of the deaf.

Vatican II thus recognized that a whole new approach to non-Catholic Christians needed to be tried. Centuries of separation amounted to just that: separation. There was no movement in inter-Christian relations; there was only a stalemate; there was stagnation. In laying out a new approach to the ecumenical question, then, the Council Fathers made use of the basic idea set forth in the Council's Dogmatic Constitution on the Church, *Lumen Gentium*, namely, that while separated Christians lacked the *fullness* of the faith and of the means of salvation in Christ, in their various Churches and communions, in varying degrees, there were nevertheless also to be found "many elements of sanctification and truth" (LG 8).

Separated Christians were thus not entirely "in error," as they had been typically regarded up to that point. Rather, they possessed at least *some* of the elements of Christian *truth* — some Bible Christians believed in Jesus perhaps even more fervently than many Catholics, for example. And most of them possessed at least some of the sacramental means of sanctification, if only baptism. For the Council Fathers, therefore, it became a question of trying to look at the glass not as half empty, but as one-quarter, one-half, or even possibly three-quarters *full*.

Vatican II's new approach was that, like the Good Shepherd in the parable, the Church herself henceforth had to *go out in search of the lost sheep* (cf. Mt 18:12). The end result of adopting this new approach to the problem of continuing Christian disunity was the Council's Decree on Ecumenism, *Unitatis Redintegratio*, which we must shortly examine in greater detail. But first we must look a bit more closely at the steps followed by the Church in her new venture in ecumenism.

CHAPTER TWO

GETTING FROM HERE TO THERE

LTHOUGH THE APPROACH by the Church to non-Catholic Christians outside her visible boundaries adumbrated by the Second Vatican Council was new, we should not imagine that it was radically "untraditional" in traditional Catholic terms. The "tradition" of passively waiting for the "return" of erring and separated brethren was actually quite recent in the perspective of the long history of the Church. It may have been a very *understandable* stance, especially considering the hardening of positions that took place on both sides following the breach of Church unity brought about by the Protestant Reformation. But it was hardly the only approach the Church had ever taken towards Christians who had unfortunately seen fit to separate themselves from her.

The historical record shows, in fact, that the Church has many times tried to reopen the dialogue with separated Christians in order to heal breaks that had occurred, notably in the case of the Eastern Orthodox after the schism of 1054. We should recall the Second Council of Lyons in 1274, for example, as well as the Council of Florence, which wound up around 1445. In these approaches, the Holy See showed itself prepared to compromise on certain non-essentials in order to achieve reunion, for example, on the status of the See of Constantinople and on the Eastern Patriarchates. Similarly, in the case of the Protestants, the Church repeatedly tried to keep the dialogue with them alive. But as decades and then centuries followed these breaches, positions on all sides inevitably did harden.

By the time of the First Vatican Council, the idea was pretty firmly established on the Catholic side that what was primarily at issue was the necessary return of those who had become separated from the true Church. Blessed Pope Pius IX, fifteen months before Vatican I, in 1868, wrote to all the Eastern Orthodox patriarchs and bishops inviting them to attend the upcoming council. He even said that they could attend *as* validly ordained bishops! Yet not a single Eastern Orthodox bishop, however, did attend; nor did a single one of them even respond to the pope's letter. It did not help that the text of the pope's letter had been leaked to the press before any of the Orthodox bishops had received their copies of it in the mail; to some Orthodox it seemed almost like a calculated put-down or insult; then, as now, the Catholic Church's public relations apparatus was not always what it should have been.

Blessed Pope Pius IX also invited various communions of Protestants and other non-Catholics to consider the upcoming ecumenical council as a possible occasion to decide to return to the one, true Catholic fold. Again, this approach proved to be quite ineffective — and actually even offensive — to most of the separated Christians and ecclesial communities invited, none of which took up the pope on his offer to attend. The divisions had become too deep-seated, and seemed now to be a permanent feature of a divided Christianity. The sad fact of these divisions formed the background of the statements made by such popes as Leo XIII and Pius XI calling for the "return" of these separated Christian communions to the true fold.

Blessed Pope John XXIII, however, who became pope in 1958, thought that these Christian divisions were scandalous. As a member of the Vatican diplomatic service, he had lived for a number of years among the Eastern Orthodox, first in Bulgaria and then in Turkey, and had come to have great respect and even affection for the Eastern Orthodox Christians. After he became pope, it was probably no surprise to those who knew him when he very prominently made a new quest for Christian unity one of his three main reasons for convoking the Second Vatican Council. This ecumenical council, the 21st in the series of councils in the long history of the Church, took place over four successive years between 1962 and 1965. The other two reasons given by John XXIII for convoking it, as he stated so eloquently in his famous Opening Address to the Council, were: the renewal of the Church's faith, and the adaptation (or updating) of her discipline and practices to meet the needs and conditions of the present day — an aim which came to be expressed by the Italian word, *aggiornamento*, or bringing up to date.

Because the pontiff placed such a marked emphasis on ecumenism as a principal means to achieve Christian reunion, John XXIII established in 1960, during preparations for the upcoming ecumenical council, a special Secretariat for Promoting Christian Unity. Its purpose, as he stated at the time, was "to show in a special manner our love and good will towards those who bear the name of Christ, but are separated from this Apostolic See, and in order that they may be able to follow the work of the Council and find more readily the way to attain that unity for which Jesus besought his heavenly Father." John XXIII placed at the head of this new Secretariat for Promoting Christian Unity Cardinal Augustin Bea, S.J., a highly respected German biblical scholar.

Cardinal Bea was destined to play a major role in more ways than one at the Second Vatican Council after it convened. John XXIII's liberal biographer, the late Peter Hebblethwaite, the English Vaticanologist, himself a former Jesuit, even wrote in his *Pope John XXIII: Shepherd of the Modern World*, that this appointment of Cardinal Bea to head this new Secretariat was "the most important appointment of his pontificate." "Without Bea," Hebblethwaite opined, "it is unlikely that Pope John would have got the Council he wanted." This was undoubtedly somewhat of an exaggeration, but there was more than a grain of truth in it nevertheless: Cardinal Bea was a member in good standing of the group of Northern European bishops and theologians who came to dominate the Second Vatican

Council, as most of the histories of the Council have recorded. In a number of ways, Cardinal Bea acted as a kind of catalyst to bring together some of the elements that ultimately made Vatican II what it was. From the outset, the new Secretariat headed by him was given a status equal to that of the regular conciliar Commissions.

Through this new Secretariat for Promoting Christian Unity, invitations to send representatives to the Council went out to Anglican, Old Catholic, Orthodox, and Protestant Churches and communions. The response was quite gratifying, unlike the response to the invitations sent nearly a century before for Vatican Council I. The ecumenical climate and outlook *had* changed. And a large number of observers from Protestant denominations eventually did attend the Council as observers — Baptists, Evangelicals, Lutherans, Reformed, Presbyterians, Friends, Disciples of Christ, Methodists, and yet others. A delegation from the Church of England was also named.

Suddenly, most non-Catholic Christian Churches and ecclesial communities *were* intensely interested in what the Catholic Church was doing. Moreover, many of them had come around to see the Catholic Church as at least in some sense legitimately "Christian," rather than being considered "the anti-Christ," or "the Whore of Babylon," of classic anti-Catholic polemics.

Initially, though, there was some confusion about the invitations to the Eastern Orthodox. The ecumenical patriarch of Constantinople was invited to assemble a delegation from the fifteen or so national Eastern Orthodox Churches in communion with him. He proved unable to do so, however, and he even failed to send a representative of his own until the Third Session in 1964. As a result, a number of Eastern Orthodox Churches were never represented at the Council at all.

Meanwhile, though, through a separate and complicated series of maneuvers, the Russian Orthodox Church was invited separately and did send a delegation. So did most of the Ancient Churches of the East not in communion with either the patriarch of Constantinople or the bishop of Rome: *inter alia,* the Armenian Apostolic Church, the Coptic Orthodox Church, the Ethiopian Orthodox Church, and the Syrian Orthodox Church. Blessed John XXIII was to order that all these observers at the Council should be seated in a prominent place of honor across from the Roman cardinals in the *aula* of St. Peter's.

This demonstration of active interest on the part of so many Christian Churches and ecclesial communities in what the Catholic Church was attempting to do in order to renew herself, though, was quite simply unprecedented. Among other things, it meant that many of these Christian bodies, no less than the Catholic Church herself, had a renewed interest in ecumenism — in *responding* to Christ's prayer "that they may all be one." The Protestant communions had mostly been active among themselves in an organized ecumenical movement that had been going on since 1910 — a movement into which both the Anglicans and Orthodox had become drawn, but which, as we have noted, the Catholic Church (especially, Pope Pius XI) had expressly declined to join.

However, around the same time that this new ecumenical ferment came to the surface in the Catholic Church with the convocation of Vatican II, it became clear that similar hopes and aspirations were welling up within other communions as well. The Eastern Orthodox Churches in communion with the ecumenical patriarch in Istanbul, for example, convoked four pan-Orthodox conferences which were roughly contemporaneous with Vatican II (in 1961, 1962, 1964, and 1968). These conferences dealt among other topics with Orthodox participation in the ecumenical movement and theological dialogue with the Catholic Church. These meetings and studies have continued among the Orthodox, culminating in the 1990s with meetings of the Orthodox primates of the various Orthodox Churches.

All of these developments, and yet others that we could cite, pointed to a conclusion that the new era of ecumenism inaugurated by the Catholic Church at Vatican II was actually being echoed in other Churches and communions. A new ecumenical breeze was blowing, as it still is, in fact, with the end result of all the new ecumenical efforts and initiatives yet to come. It is really premature, in other words, if not actually short-sighted, to decide that, just because no actual instances of Christian reunification have yet occurred, Vatican II was therefore mistaken in its strong ecumenical aim and thrust.

Similarly, Vatican II's key idea that the Church must now pro-actively reach out to separated Christians if we are to expect any real movement towards genuine Christian unity — this idea was hardly new. As the great Saint Augustine wrote in his Discourse on Psalm 33, we must instead:

> "...have charity, not only for one another, but also for those who are outside the Church. Of these, some are still pagans who have not yet made an act of faith in Christ. Others are separated, insofar as they are joined with us in professing faith in Christ, our head, but are yet divided from the unity of his body. My friends, we must grieve over these as over our own brothers. *Whether they like it or not, they are our brothers; and they will only cease to be so when they no longer say, 'Our Father...'*"
> (emphasis added).

This, then, was the fundamental decision Vatican Council II made about those Christians and Christian bodies separated from the unity of the Catholic Church, namely, that they *are* our brothers, "whether they like it or not"; and that the Church therefore had a responsibility to go out pro-actively in search of the unity for which Christ prayed. It was a point of view that had been neglected for a long time, but it was no less true for all of that. One of the results of it was, as things turned out, that the Catholic Church, in effect, *took over the leadership of the world ecumenical movement*! That, in fact, is about where things still stand today.

CHAPTER THREE

THE DEBATES ON ECUMENISM
AT THE COUNCIL

EVEN THOUGH the new ecumenism inaugurated at Vatican II
fits well within the overall Catholic tradition, properly understood, it nevertheless represented a genuinely new departure for the Fathers of the Council who had all grown up and
been formed in the era of Pope Pius XI's *Mortalium Animos*, which
simply envisaged, as we have seen, a "return" of erring Christian
brethren to the true Church of Christ. This fact was reflected in the
conciliar debates on the conciliar *schema* which eventually became
the Decree on Ecumenism, *Unitatis Redintegratio*. There were spir-
ited and even highly critical interventions in the debates about ecumenism which took place at the Council and which finally resulted
in the drawing up and approval of this Decree on Ecumenism itself.

Actually, in the beginning, there were three documents which
were combined to form the basis of the eventual Decree: there was
a *schema* on Church unity which had been drawn up by the Preparatory Commission for the Oriental [Catholic] Churches headed
by Cardinal Amleto Cicognani, then Vatican Secretary of State;
there was a chapter entitled "On Ecumenism" in the initial *schema*,
De Ecclesia (which eventually became *Lumen Gentium*) prepared
by the Theological Preparatory Commission headed by Cardinal

Alfredo Ottaviani, then head of what was at the time called the Congregation of the Holy Office (today the Congregation for the Doctrine of the Faith); and finally, there was yet another *schema* drafted by Cardinal Augustin Bea's new Secretariat for Promoting Christian Unity.

Technically, only the first of these three documents ever reached the Council floor for debate during the First Session in 1962; but the other documents were known to have been circulated widely among the bishops and their *periti*, or theological experts and advisors. And so when speaker after speaker during the debate mentioned that the three documents should be combined into one, it became clear that that was how the Fathers wished to handle the matter. No one of the three documents, by itself, really set forth the kind of new ecumenism that would eventually emerge.

The draft prepared by Cardinal Cicognani's Preparatory Commission was written from the point of view of the Eastern Catholic Churches already in communion with the Holy See. However important they were to the overall Catholicity of the Church, these Churches were not necessarily the fittest instruments with which to approach the Eastern Orthodox Churches, since their very existence often tended to be a very sore point with the latter. In the end, the Council decided to issue a separate Decree on the Eastern Catholic Churches, *Orientalium Eccclesiarum,* regulating the status of these Churches within the overall framework of the "universal" Catholic Church, of which the Latin or Roman "rite" is by far the largest unit worldwide, though in fact it is not the only one. Far from it. Rather, within the Catholic Church there are some twenty or more existing Eastern Catholic Churches divided among ecclesial traditions labeled Alexandrian, Antiochian, Armenian, Byzantine, and Chaldean. Relatively small in the number of their members today, these Eastern Catholic Churches nevertheless represent venerable and authentic historical traditions, some of them going back to the beginnings of Christianity.

Given the existence and flourishing of all these Eastern Catholic Churches, it is actually a misnomer to refer to the Catholic Church as the *Roman* Catholic Church. The "Roman" component is only a part, though a very large part, of the worldwide communion in question. But the proper name of Christ's Church is simply "the Catholic Church," the name she has borne since the first century.

The conciliar *schema* "On Ecumenism," prepared by Cardinal Alfredo Ottaviani's Theological Preparatory Commission, dealt with those Churches and communions separated from the Catholic Church. This *schema* contained a discussion of the general principles of ecumenism from the Catholic perspective; but like many of the drafts prepared by the curial Preparatory Commissions for the Council, this draft was considered, especially by the bishops in the dominant European Alliance, to be quite inadequate for the times. This was one of the reasons why these particular bishops wanted to see this document combined with the other two drafts: they wanted it to be absorbed by them. The draft prepared by Cardinal Bea's Christian Unity Secretariat, on the other hand, did not yet enjoy the prestige that the productions of this body would enjoy later on at the Council.

The upshot of all this was that on December 1, 1962, the Council decided by an overwhelming vote of 2,068 to 36 that all three of the existing drafts should be combined into a single *schema* with the title, *De Oecumenismo*. A special joint commission composed of representatives from all three of the interested bodies — now dominated by the Secretariat for the Promotion of Christian Unity — were instructed to prepare a combined draft which would be considered the following year during the Second Session in 1963. This draft consisted of five chapters, of which the final two dealt with the questions of the Jews and of religious liberty, respectively. It soon became clear, though, that these last two chapters would have to be detached entirely from the *schema* on ecumenism; in the end, they would form the basis of the Council's two later separate documents on non-Christian religions and on religious liberty, respectively; but they remained part of the *schema* on ecumenism while it was being debated. The debate as such occupied the last two weeks of the Second Session from November 18 to December 2, 1963. The *schema* was introduced by Cardinal Joseph Martin of Rouen, France, who observed that:

> The spirit of the *schema* is pacific and irenic. The ecumenical question is altogether new, for it responds to a new situation. Divisions among Christians today are a cause of scandal to those who are unbelievers. They paralyze the work of evangelization. This is a fact of daily experience.

The terms of the debate on *De Oecumenismo* were not always clear-cut, since some of the speakers were addressing questions related to the document's chapters on the Jews or religious liberty. The American bishops, for example, were primarily interested in this latter subject, especially as it related to the Church's situation in the United States, where the idea of "the separation of Church and state" held such sway. Nevertheless, the American bishops were solidly in favor of new ecumenical initiatives as well.

Speaking in the name of all the American bishops, Cardinal Joseph Ritter of St. Louis delivered a major intervention in the debate on ecumenism in which he placed the Church in America squarely behind a renewed quest for Christian unity. Consideration of this topic by the Council, he said, "responds to the *aggiornamento* urged by John XXIII and Paul VI [and] rings the death knell of the Counter-Reformation." There was a duty to hasten the day of unity by prayer and study, he thought. Dialogue with those outside the Church was essential, based on the freedom of the act of faith, the inviolability of the human conscience, and the incompetence of the civil government to interpret the Gospel of Christ. Since the Eucharist was necessarily the center of unity, greater attention should be paid to the validity of the sacraments and orders of the Eastern Orthodox Churches. Nothing offensive to Protestants should be decreed. Nor, he thought, should anyone hesitate to apply the term "Church" to separated Christian bodies. According to the St. Louis prelate, a guide or directory for ecumenical affairs was badly needed (which, in fact, the Council would mandate, and the first part of a Directory of Ecumenical Affairs would be published as early as 1967).

This attitude of openness on the part of the American bishops to a new ecumenism was typical of a majority of the bishops at the Council. A new wind was indeed blowing on this subject. Cardinal Paul-Émile Léger of Montreal expressed this openness by saying that "the present hope for and movement towards unity are not passing impulses but are inspired by the Gospel and the Holy Spirit. We are fearful when we realize what a burden of history we must overcome," he went on. "But we must face the task of dialogue with positive and truly Catholic prudence." This sentiment was echoed by Cardinal Franz König of Vienna, who observed that "we should avoid any impression that Catholic ecumenism is a closed and perfect system. We are only at the beginning. The dialogue, together with prayer and the Holy Spirit, may lead us to new aspects and a more profound understanding of ecumenism." Cardinal König was destined to play a significant role in ecumenical affairs in the postconciliar era through the Pro Oriente Foundation which he established in 1964 as a project of the archdiocese of Vienna to develop better relations with the Eastern Churches. One of the giants of Vatican II, Cardinal König lived until March, 2004, when he died at age 98, the last surviving cardinal who had been named by Blessed Pope John XXIII.

The strong-minded Melchite Catholic Patriarch, the 87-year-old Maximos IV Saigh, probably convinced many of the waverers that the new direction the Council was headed in was indeed the right direction. He noted that the *schema* on ecumenism deserved more than mere assent; it was outstanding, he thought, both in its doctrinal profundity and in its pastoral orientation. According to him, the *schema* eschewed useless polemics and easy proselytism, and instead favored honest dialogue based on truth. He thought that the document's theology of the Church would resonate with the Eastern Orthodox Churches; and he made specific reference in this connection to the most recent Pan-Orthodox conference on the island of Rhodes, which had taken place around that same time. Like many of the Council Fathers, however, this Melchite Patriarch favored dropping Chapter IV on the Jews and Chapter V on religious liberty. Coming from the Middle East, as he did, he believed that the question of the Muslims had to be addressed by the Council, every bit as much as that of the Jews; but, he thought, this particular *schema* was not the place to do it. Ecumenism, in any case, he thought, primarily concerned the relationships of Christians among themselves. There was substantial sentiment in favor of the new ecumenical thrust that Vatican II would in fact adopt.

However, it was not the case that there was no opposition to *De Oecumenismo*, especially at first. On the contrary, there was considerable opposition, as well as no little apprehension, concerning the new tack the Council was now taking. The Council was obviously turning 180 degrees away from the former philosophy of simply expecting a "return" of Christians who were separated from the Catholic Church and were hence by definition considered to be mired "in error." But the Council was embarked on a new and unfamiliar road leading to an unexplored destination. Enough opposition was expressed in the course of the debate, in fact, that some strong proponents of the *schema* feared that it might even be dropped as inopportune. The excision of the last two chapters on the Jews and religious liberty was even proposed, in part, in order to save the substance of the new ecumenism and allow it to appear independently in a Council document.

Typical of the kind of opposition that was expressed in the debate were the interventions of two Spanish cardinals, Benjamin Arriba y Castro, archbishop of Tarragona, and Jósé Bueno Monreal, archbishop of Seville. The latter feared that the schema might appear to sanction a kind of pan-Christianity or religious syncretism which could lead to the sort of religious indifferentism, often condemned by the Church. The distinctiveness of the Catholic faith, the archbishop of Seville thought, needed to be maintained in the face of the errors about the faith that abounded outside the Church's boundaries.

Cardinal Arriba y Castro, for his part, was quite negative about the whole *schema* and thought that it should be dropped entirely; he said:

> We magnify the dialogue, we talk of prayer in common; this is all very fine, but let us beware of the dangers and always strictly respect the laws of the Church, such as the Index, which prohibits books favoring heresy. It is inopportune to speak of ecumenism in a council. This will scandalize the faithful of little education, who will be confused and put all churches on the same level.
>
> Proselytizing is increasing. Let us ask our separated brethren to renounce all proselytizing among Catholics. But the Church's right to preach the Gospel everywhere must be recognized. Let us insist on charity towards our separated brethren but first of all our fidelity to Christ. This *schema* does not please me. It is very badly done. It is better to avoid such a subject altogether. A secretariat for unity, which works directly under the pope, is enough.

These views of the archbishop of Tarragona were not unrepresentative of some of the thinking of the time; and they obviously reflected the very familiar view of the day that "error has no rights." This was an idea that would surface again when the Council debated the specific question of religious liberty in the later sessions. There can be no doubt that the Spanish prelate's viewpoint was shared by not a few of his fellow Council Fathers.

Nevertheless, the upshot of the debate on ecumenism during the Second Session in 1963 was basically that the Church should indeed move forward with an ecumenical initiative; the draft schema was to be revised in the light of the debate; and the chapters on the Jews and religious liberty were to be excised and treated separately in separate conciliar documents. It was expected that the final document on ecumenism would be debated and approved during the Third Session of the Council in 1964.

By that time, a year later, however, there were multiple stresses and strains in the Council. There was the continuing debate about episcopal collegiality, for example — the necessary cooperation that must take place among the Catholic bishops with one another and with their head bishop, the pope. As a result of these stresses and strains, Pope Paul VI felt obliged to intervene with his significant *Nota Explicativa Praevia* in order to secure the near unanimous approval of the Dogmatic Constitution on the Church, *Lumen Gentium*, that was so badly needed if the document was to be considered an authentic expression of the mind and will of the Council. This *Nota Praevia* of Pope Paul VI was appended to the text of *Lumen Gentium*, not without some dissatisfaction on the part of some of the bishops, who did not think the pope should intervene so directly in the work of the Council. The pope, however, was seeking to arrive at an authentic consensus on the part of the vast majority of the bishops present at the Council.

We have already taken note of the fact that the new ecumenism was *based* on the teaching of *Lumen Gentium* that while the Catholic Church possesses the *fullness* of the truth and graces of Christ, those Christian bodies separated from the Church are not necessarily deprived of some measure of that truth and those graces which belong to Christ. Approval of the earlier conciliar document, *Lumen Gentium*, was thus essential to the validity of any subsequent approval of the Decree on Ecumenism, *Unitatis Redintegratio.*

There was also the whole very large issue of religious liberty, which by then had emerged on its own in a full-blown *schema* for which the U.S. bishops, in particular, were strenuously lobbying. Their belief, shared by many others, was that although religious liberty was now in a *schema* separate from the ecumenism schema, the credibility of the latter nevertheless depended heavily on the stated intention of the Council to affirm the principles of religious liberty, particularly the principle that, even though "error had no rights," human beings, human persons, *did* have rights, specifically a right to the freedom of their consciences in matters of religion. Much to the chagrin of the American bishops, though, the preliminary vote on the topic of religious liberty was postponed in 1964 until the following year. The fear was that if the vote were postponed, the *schema* would be abandoned (this fear proved to be unfounded in the end).

In the midst of the turmoil that characterized the closing days of the Third Session of the Council, in 1964, the completed *schema De Oecumenismo* too became the subject of a direct papal intervention, and thereby underwent a number of last minute changes. The Council's Secretary General, Archbishop Pericle Felici, blandly announced that nineteen changes had been made by "higher authority" — which meant, of course, that the pope had intervened. These changes by "higher authority" were intended, it was stated, to make the exact meaning of the text clearer. Even so, the idea of any direct papal intervention in the work of the Council continued to be opposed by some of the bishops, as well as by the (generally liberal) observers of the proceedings of the Council. Nevertheless, Archbishop Felici read aloud the changes proposed by Pope Paul VI to the assembled Council Fathers. Substantively, they were not all that significant, mostly just qualifying or toning down some of the more direct statements in the text; many of them consisted only of the addition of adverbs. Pope Paul VI, by general agreement, almost always took a rather "nuanced" approach to whatever question he felt obliged to address as the supreme pontiff.

For example, in one place, the pope directed that the word "Catholic" be inserted before the word "Church" in a sentence that spoke of "the fullness of grace and truth entrusted to the Catholic Church" (UR 3). Again, in the same numbered section of the text, the pope had inserted the phrase "in its members" following "the people" constituting the Church as being still liable to sin — so that it could not be predicated of the holy Church herself that *she* was liable to sin, but only in her members!

Some of the Protestant observers detected an anti-Protestant slant in these changes inserted by Pope Paul VI. Some of these same observers, along with some of the bishops themselves, also resented the way changes were being introduced into a conciliar text by "higher authority." Such a direct papal intervention in the conciliar process was considered improper and not in accordance with the Council's own rules (but then *all* of the Council's decisions and documents ultimately remained subject to the approval and ratification of the supreme pontiff).

However, Pope Paul VI may have decided to intervene in order to placate the minority at the Council that still either opposed or at any rate was apprehensive about the Council's adoption of the new ecumenism. The changes he wanted were in some cases identical to suggestions which some members of the minority had already unsuccessfully tried to persuade Cardinal Bea's Secretariat to adopt. The consistent policy of Paul VI at Vatican II was to try to insure as many favorable votes as possible in order to establish the authority of the finished Decree as an official document of the Church's conciliar magisterium. Catholics believe, of course, that the final, formal teachings of an ecumenical council are guaranteed by the Holy Spirit, and hence it cannot be discounted that perhaps the Holy Spirit too wished to see some of these changes and nuances contained in the final, approved Decree on Ecumenism that were included by means of the intervention of "higher authority," namely, the pope himself. However that may be, a unanimous or near unanimous vote by the Catholic bishops in council has traditionally been taken as strong evidence of the presence of the guiding Holy Spirit in the decisions of the council in question.

The final vote on the Decree on Ecumenism, *Unitatis Redintegratio*, which took place on November 21, 1964, recorded 2,137 episcopal votes in favor, and only 11 bishops opposed. This was exactly the kind of result which Pope Paul VI constantly sought in the course of Vatican Council II.

After not a few uncertainties and even vicissitudes, then, the Catholic Church was now officially on record in favor of the new ecumenism. It was a major step, and one of the most significant decreed by the Second Vatican Council.

CHAPTER FOUR

THE DECREE ON ECUMENISM
UNITATIS REDINTEGRATIO

WHAT KIND OF DOCUMENT is the Decree on Ecumenism, *Unitatis Redintegratio,* as it was finally approved by the Council and promulgated by the pope? One of the distinguished Protestant observers at the Council, Dr. Oscar Cullmann — who was not always automatically favorable to the Council's work — described it as "more than the opening of a door; new ground has been broken. No Catholic document has ever spoken of non-Catholic Christians in this way." If the Council truly intended to break new ground on ecumenism, it certainly succeeded, in the eyes of this prominent Protestant observer.

The very first sentence in the Introduction to the text declares that "the restoration of unity among Christians is one of the principal concerns of the Second Vatican Council." The second sentence is no less definite in stating that "Christ the Lord founded one Church and one Church only." The text does not directly or immediately draw the obvious conclusion that all the followers of Christ therefore ought to be members of that one Church that Christ founded, if indeed such a Church is still to be found in the world (Catholics, of course, believe that such a Church *is* indeed still to be found in the world!). Instead, the text immediately points to the fact of division among Christians and mentions "the many Christian communions" all presenting themselves "as true inheritors of Jesus Christ."

"Such division," the text goes on to say, and quite emphatically, "openly contradicts the will of Christ, scandalizes the world, and
damages that most holy cause, the preaching of the Gospel to every
creature" (UR 1). The document makes clear that the ecumenism it
is speaking of is an affair between and among Christians, whom it
defines as all those "who invoke the Triune God and confess Jesus
as Lord and Savior" (UR 1). "Christian" thus means "Trinitarian" as
well as "Christocentric," according to the Second Vatican Council.

The first three chapters of the much debated draft *De Oecumenismo* survive in the three chapters that make up the final text of
the Decree. The first chapter is entitled "Catholic Principles on Ecumenism" — *not* "Principles of Catholic Ecumenism," by the way,
as was the case in the first draft. The change implies a recognition
that ecumenism is for all Christian Churches and communions, each
of which might then have its own particular principles regarding
ecumenism, as does the Catholic Church in this Decree. And so the
principles which the Church does have necessarily *are* "Catholic"
principles.

The second chapter covers "The Practice of Ecumenism,"
while the third chapter discusses "Churches and Ecclesial Communities Separated from the Roman Apostolic See." The document
is not a lengthy one. Nevertheless, it concisely and economically
treats all the essential points. In terms of the number of follow-up
post-Vatican II documents inspired by it or produced in its wake,
this Decree comes in second among the Documents of Vatican II.
It is second only to the Constitution on the Sacred Liturgy, *Sac-
rosanctum Concilium*. Ecumenism thus *has* been a major concern
and preoccupation of the Catholic Church in the post-conciliar era;
it is *not* just a minor or side issue as far as the official stance of the
Church is concerned.

No doubt because of the misgivings and actual fears of many
of the Council Fathers that an uncritical, unprincipled, or overly enthusiastic type of ecumenism could lead to religious indifferentism
and to the downgrading of the truths of the faith, at least in some

minds, the text very quickly proceeds to make clear that the Catholic Church, while fervently desiring the unity of all Christians, has nevertheless in no way relinquished her traditional claim to be "the one Church and the one Church only" founded by Jesus Christ.

After a brief Scripture-based account of the foundation of the Church upon Peter and the other apostles — including references to the three famous Petrine scriptural passages in Matthew 16, Luke 22, and John 21 — the text proceeds in various ways to underline the essential oneness of Christ's Church, referring to her as "God's only flock" (UR 2), and as the "one and only Church of God" (UR 3). It is in the following statement, however, that the Catholic Church's continuing claim to be the one, true Church of Christ is expressed more clearly and eloquently than anywhere else in all the Documents of Vatican II:

> For it is through Christ's Catholic Church alone, which is the universal help towards salvation, that the fullness of the means of salvation can be obtained. It was to the apostolic college alone, of which Peter is the head, that we believe that Our Lord entrusted all the blessings of the New Covenant, in order to establish on earth the one Body of Christ into which all those should be fully incorporated who belong in any way to the people of God (UR 3).

It is perhaps more than a little ironic that Vatican II's strongest and most insistent reiteration of the Church's traditional claim to be the one, true Church founded by Jesus Christ should have come, of all places, in its Decree on Ecumenism. Yet the same text goes on to speak further of "the unity of the one and only Church," which, echoing *Lumen Gentium,* the text specifies that "we believe *subsists* in the Catholic Church as something she can never lose" (UR 4); emphasis added).

Thus, there can be no question but that the Second Vatican Council plainly and definitely reiterated the traditional teaching of

the Catholic Church to the effect that she herself is the one, true
Church of Christ. If some, nevertheless, in the years after the Council, *did*, nevertheless, as a result of an uncritical, unprincipled, or
overly enthusiastic type of ecumenism, allow their faith to be weakened in this regard, or even fell into the kind of religious indifferentism that some of the Council Fathers feared — and we surely have
to grant that this kind of thing unfortunately *has* been an occasional
feature of the post-conciliar era on the part of some — this can nevertheless *not* be attributed to the teaching of *Unitatis Redintegratio*
as such. For, as we have now seen, this Vatican II document plainly
and firmly held that the Catholic Church is the one, true Church of
Christ.

Since the subject of the Decree is ecumenism, however, that
is, the relations between and among separated Christians, the text of
the Decree goes on to point out how Christians and Christian communions outside the visible communion of the Catholic Church do
not enjoy the "fullness" of the means of salvation which the Catholic
Church alone enjoys. Indeed, the "differences that exist… whether
in doctrine and sometimes in discipline — or concerning the structure of the Church — do indeed create many obstacles, sometimes
serious ones, to full ecclesiastical communion" (UR 4).

Still, the tone of the document remains positive, and "all who
have been justified by faith in baptism" are held to have been "incorporated into Christ," at least in some measure. Moreover, in an
extremely important psychological concession by the Church —
this was surely necessary if there is ever to be any real ecumenical
progress in the practical order — the text plainly says: "One cannot
charge with the sin of separation those who at present are born into
[separate] communities and in them are brought up in the faith of
Christ.… The Catholic Church accepts them with respect and affection as brothers.… Often enough," the text specifies, "men on both
sides were to blame" (*Ibid.*).

The text then elaborates on *Lumen Gentium* in listing some of
the "elements and endowments which… can exist outside the visible

boundaries of the Catholic Church: the written Word of God; the life of grace; faith, hope, and charity, with the other interior gifts of the Holy Spirit; as well as visible elements — all of which 'come from Christ and lead back to him', [and] belong by right to the Church of Christ" (UR 4). Nevertheless, whatever truths and means of grace they might possess, "our separated brethren, whether considered as individuals, or as communities and Churches, are not blessed with that unity which Jesus Christ wished to bestow on all those to whom he has given new birth into one body" (*Ibid.*).

In other words, it is Christ who desires Christian unity; it is Christ who prayed that "they may all be one" (Jn 17:20). In view of this, the Catholic Church must renew efforts to help create the conditions that could again make unity possible. In order to do this, the text identifies several actions to which Christians on all sides should be dedicated:

- Every effort should be made "to avoid expressions, judgments, and actions which do not represent the condition of our separated brethren with truth and fairness."
- Dialogue should be carried on "between competent experts from different Churches and communities… [in which] each explains the teaching of his communion in greater depth and brings out clearly its distinctive features."
- All Christians should cooperate more diligently in carrying out works "for the common good of humanity which are demanded by the Christian conscience."
- All Christians should more often "come together for common prayer where this is permitted."
- All Christians should "examine their own faithfulness to Christ's will for the Church and, wherever necessary, undertake with vigor the task of renewal and reform" (UR 4).

In the second chapter of *Unitatis Redintegratio* entitled "The Practice of Ecumenism," the text points out that "every renewal of the Church essentially consists of an increase of fidelity to her own calling," recognizing that "as an institution of men here on earth... if there have been deficiencies in moral conduct or in Church discipline — or even in the way that Church teaching has been formulated" — these errors and shortcomings must be "carefully distinguished from the deposit of faith itself" (UR 6).

In speaking thus of "deficiencies," even possibly "in the way that Church teaching has been formulated," the text comes close, in the opinion of some critics, to saying that the Church's magisterium might possibly have sometimes been *wrong*. In the wake of the loss of confidence in Church teaching on the part of so many Catholics that arose in the post-conciliar era, especially as a result of the widespread public dissent from Pope Paul VI's encyclical *Humanae Vitae* on birth control issued in 1968, this criticism may seem plausible. Some over-eager Catholics *have* sometimes been willing to minimize doctrine in the supposed interest of ecumenical advancement. Yet it should be pointed out that the conciliar text itself carefully distinguishes between possible mistakes by Churchmen and "the deposit of faith itself." In other words, the text, in effect, reaffirms the Church's traditional belief that the deposit of faith, as presented by the Church, has consistently enjoyed, and enjoys, the special protection of the Holy Spirit. The Council is able to admit to "deficiencies" precisely because "the deposit of faith" itself is safe and secure, as Christ promised and as the Holy Spirit insures.

Another passage from this second chapter of the Decree which has sometimes been misinterpreted and even exploited by dissenters in the post-conciliar period, by the way, is the statement in UR 11 that when doctrines are being discussed and compared in ecumenical dialogue, it needs to be remembered that "in Catholic doctrine there exists an order or 'hierarchy' of truths, since they vary in their relation to the foundation of the Christian faith." Some have incorrectly seized upon this concept of a hierarchy of truths to imply or even assert that some truths of the faith are perhaps *less true* than some other teachings (or perhaps they are not even true at all!). This misinterpretation of UR 11 has been advanced to justify dissent from unpopular teachings which dissenters would like to downplay or presumably get rid of entirely. If such teachings are farther down in the hierarchy of truths, some imagine, then perhaps they *are* less true, or, at any rate, less important, and thus they presumably do *not* have to be believed or followed — or perhaps proposed to non-Catholics in ecumenical dialogue.

It should go without saying, of course, that the Catholic teaching prohibiting recourse to modern birth control methods is one of the teachings that many would like to see laid aside as perhaps less important or "less true" than the Church's teachings concerning, say, the Incarnation, the Resurrection, or the Real Presence of Jesus Christ in the Eucharist. A proper understanding of the principle of UR 11 should, however, and needless to say, do preclude any such improper interpretation of the anti-birth control teaching as being somehow lower down in the hierarchy of truths and therefore expendable.

But UR 11 expressly characterizes all such teachings as "truths" — that is, they are all equally *true.* To be ranked farther down in the hierarchy of truths simply means that they are farther from the foundation or center of the revealed truths of the faith such as the Trinity, the Incarnation, the Resurrection, the Real Presence, and so on. And also they may only be *derived* from revealed truths, for example, rather than being directly revealed themselves. In this sense, and in this sense alone, perhaps they are "secondary," as is the case with some of the Church's moral teachings. Nevertheless, they are no less than the primary truths also *true* — and they are also necessary to the integrity of the faith, which remains a seamless garment, even while some threads may be found on its edges while others are in the center of the fabric. The idea of hierarchy of truths as set forth in this chapter, then, does *not* justify dissent from Church teaching, though it may be easy enough to understand why someone determined upon dissent might seize upon the concept from UR 11 in order to try to claim Vatican II's sanction for the dissent in question.

The remainder of this second chapter of the Decree on Ecumenism is pretty straightforward. Great emphasis is placed upon ecumenical dialogue between Christians in different Churches and communities, as well as upon the accurate presentation to each other of the various beliefs and practices of Christians. Prayer in common with separated Christians is strongly emphasized, although official, liturgical *worship* in common (*communicatio in sacris*) remains generally *forbidden*, except in some limited cases with the Eastern Orthodox. Even though Christians may pray together, actual communion in sacramental worship has not been, and cannot be, achieved, so long as unity of belief has not been agreed upon. We *cannot* lay aside, even in the interests of possible unity, the *truth* of essential Catholic teachings, and we must place that truth ahead of any possible agreement on lesser questions.

It is true that some traditionalists, in particular, have strongly and even bitterly criticized the idea of simple prayer in common, as if it somehow *were* sacramental worship. The Council Fathers were surely correct, however, in assuming that the faithful would need to use their heads about such things, and make the proper distinctions and judgments. If there was to be even the beginning of any discussion among Christians of the differences in doctrine and discipline which continue to separate them from each other, they obviously had to agree that they had at least something in common: common prayer was thus a good place to start, in fact. In itself, it compromises nobody's positions. We can *always* pray together, even while we leave possible agreement on other issues to another time and place.

In the presentation of *doctrine*, though, *Unitatis Redintegratio* specifies that "it is essential that the doctrine be clearly presented in its entirety. Nothing is so foreign to the spirit of ecumenism," the document goes on to add, "as a false irenicism which harms the purity of Catholic doctrine and obscures its genuine and certain meaning" (UR 11).

The third chapter of the Decree is entitled "Churches and Ecclesial Communities Separated from the Roman Apostolic See," and it very generally, though quite precisely, describes those with whom the ecumenical dialogue is to be conducted:

> The first divisions occurred in the East, either because of the dispute over the dogmatic formulae of the Councils of Ephesus and Chalcedon, or later by the dissolving of ecclesiastical communion between the Eastern Patriarchates and the Roman See.
>
> Still other divisions arose in the West more than four centuries later. These stemmed from the events which are commonly referred to as the Reformation. As a result, many communions, national or confessional, were separated from the Roman See. Among those in which Catholic traditions and institutions in part continue to exist, the Anglican Communion occupies a special place (UR 13).

It would be hard to describe the universe of non-Catholic Christianity any more clearly and concisely than is the case here. The text goes on to point out that "these various divisions differ greatly from one another, not only by reason of their origin, place, and time, but still more by reason of the nature and seriousness of questions concerning faith and Church order" (UR 13). Because of these obvious differences, the text treats separately the kind of approach to be made, on the one hand, to the Eastern Christian Churches, and, on the other hand, to those in the West stemming principally from the Reformation.

The fact that the Eastern Churches retain apostolic succession, a valid hierarchy and priesthood along with valid sacraments, and, for the most part, profess historical Creeds and doctrines identical to or compatible with the belief of the Catholic Church, means that these Churches can be approached on the basis of an already existing and even quite substantial "unity." However, because of the historical circumstances involved in the original breaks, as well as of those that have developed during the centuries of separation, this substantial existing unity still cannot be transformed into full unity either easily or possibly any time soon. The perceived differences are probably still too great, even if, on careful examination, they sometimes seem to be no more than "misunderstandings" or even "prejudices."

Nevertheless, in speaking of the separated Eastern Churches, the Decree on Ecumenism includes high praise for their teachings, worship, and practices. Significantly, in view of the continuing rejection of the Roman Primacy (in varying degrees by virtually all of the separated Eastern Orthodox Churches), the document specifies that "the Churches of the East, while keeping in mind the necessary unity of the whole Church, have the power to govern themselves according to their own disciplines." The text adds that these disciplines "are better suited to the character of their faithful and better adapted to foster the good of souls" (UR 16).

With respect to the desired unity which ecumenical dialogue could hopefully help bring about, the text draws its inspiration from the example of the primitive Council of Jerusalem described in the New Testament Book of Acts 15, stating that "one must impose no burden beyond what is indispensable" (UR 18). This is a significant passage since for the Eastern Churches, the fear that reunion could lead to the loss of their accustomed practices and the governance of their Churches has been one of their principal stated motives for refusing to consider reunion with the See of Rome. Sometimes they have pointed to the experience of the Eastern Churches already in communion with Rome as ample justification for their continuing refusal to consider reunion — although in recent years, especially since Vatican II, the Church has stressed the importance of maintaining the traditions of the Eastern Catholic Churches in communion with Rome, and in most respects has treated our Eastern Catholic brethren with greater sensitivity and positive concern.

As far as the separated Churches and ecclesial communities in the West are concerned, the text adopts a determinedly positive attitude, although it is recognized that there is considerably less commonality with Christian bodies which have not maintained the sacramental system intact. On the other hand, as the document points out, there is in many respects a common Western *mentality* that the Catholic Church shares with many Protestant denominations. Both Catholics and Protestants have continued to be exceptionally *missionary* minded, for example. The text points out that Protestants "are bound to the Catholic Church by a specially close relationship as a result of the long span of earlier centuries when the Christian people had lived in ecclesiastical communion" (UR 19).

"But since these Churches and ecclesial communities differ considerably not only from us but also among themselves, due to their different origins and convictions in doctrine and spiritual life, the task of describing them is extremely difficult" (*Ibid.*). Still, the Council Fathers "rejoice that our separated brethren look to Christ as the source and center of ecclesiastical communion" (UR 20). Baptism, too, "constitutes the sacramental bond of unity existing among all who through it are reborn" (UR 22).

Nevertheless, the text recognizes obstacles in the way of re-union with the Christian bodies that stem from the Reformation, even though their continuing devotion to the Lord is considered worthy of honor and is believed to form a sufficient basis for ecumenical dialogue:

> Although the ecclesial communities separated from us lack the fullness of unity with us which flows from baptism, and although we believe they have not preserved the proper reality of the Eucharistic mystery in its fullness, especially because of the absence of the sacrament of Orders, nevertheless when they commemorate the Lord's death and resurrection in the Holy Supper, they profess that it signifies life in communion with Christ and they await his coming in glory. For these reasons, the doctrine about the Lord's Supper, about the other sacraments, worship, and ministry in the Church, should form subjects of dialogue (UR 22).

Thus, in spite of obvious impediments and obstacles that stand in the way of possible reunion among separated Christians and Christian bodies, Vatican II's Decree on Ecumenism, *Unitatis Redintegratio*, remains determined to pursue the goal. It plainly recognizes that "this holy objective — the reconciliation of all Christians in the unity of the one and only Church of Christ — transcends human powers and gifts. It therefore places its hope entirely in the prayer of Christ for the Church, in the love of the Father for us, and in the power of the Holy Spirit" (UR 24).

As a practical matter, though, the Fathers of the Council obviously placed great hopes also in the success of the renewal of the Catholic Church being undertaken by the Council itself. To the extent that this renewal could prove to be successful, the Council's hopes for Christian reunion could turn out to be successful too. So it was believed. Just because this has evidently not yet occurred — more than forty years after the Council — this does not mean that the hope was vain. This remains the case for the simple reason that much still remains to be worked out, and may well still be worked out as time goes on. As we shall see, there *has* been progress since Vatican II's ecumenical quest began, even though it has not yet resulted in any actual Christian reunion.

To this end, the Council Fathers always hoped that Catholics everywhere would take part in the renewal of the Church by working on the renewal of their own faith. In the past, it was thought, Catholics had been too ready to let things ride, to let things go along in their accustomed ways. As part of the necessary renewal, this was precisely one of the attitudes that needed to be changed; the Church needed a better and more positive attitude on the part of her own sons and daughters. As the Decree on Ecumenism itself expresses it:

> For although the Catholic Church has been endowed
> with all divinely revealed truth and with all means of
> grace, yet its members fail to live by them with all the
> fervor that they should. As a result the radiance of the

Church's face shines less brightly in the eyes of our separated brethren and of the world at large, and the growth of God's kingdom is retarded. Every Catholic must therefore aim at Christian perfection and, each according to his station, play his part, that the Church, which bears in her own body the humility and dying of Jesus, may daily be more purified and renewed, against the day when Christ will present her to himself in all her glory without spot or wrinkle (UR 4).

CHAPTER FIVE

THE IMPORTANCE OF DIALOGUE: POPE PAUL VI'S *ECCLESIAM SUAM*

I N THE COURSE OF our discussion of Vatican Council II's new ecumenism, it perhaps will have been noticed that a rather dominant idea, the idea of ecumenical "dialogue," has regularly recurred. The Council Fathers made frequent reference to such dialogue in the course of their debates on ecumenism. The Decree on Ecumenism, *Unitatis Redintegratio,* itself specifically recommends it, or at least mentions it, an unusual number of times (UR 4, 9, 11, 18, 19, 21, 22 & 23). The subject is taken up again in some of the Council's later documents, for example, in the Pastoral Constitution on the Church in the Modern World, *Gaudium et Spes* (92), and in the Decree on the Church's Missionary Activity, *Ad Gentes Divinitus* (15).

Among the plethora of documents issued on the subject of ecumenism following the Council, the Secretariat for Promoting Christian Unity, on August 15, 1970, issued an important document specifically on the subject of ecumenical dialogue. Its title was: "Reflections and Suggestions concerning Ecumenical Dialogue." Few subjects, in other words, have been as assiduously discussed and promoted as has "dialogue," at and after Vatican II.

There are Catholics, of course, usually of a more traditional bent, who have never quite been able to muster the same enthusiasm for dialogue that the authorities of the Church have so strongly exhibited in the post-Vatican II era. These Catholics tend to doubt that all the new dialogue, however polite and civil, as contrasted to the earlier prejudice and suspicion that too often tended to characterize relationships among separated Christians, is really going to lead anywhere — they often point to the post-Vatican II experience, in fact, and point out that it *hasn't* led to Christian reunion! And they then further claim that the Church's actual experience since Vatican II has thus not shown that their negative view of dialogue is fundamentally mistaken. Indeed, it must be conceded that there *are* limitations on what can be accomplished in pursuing dialogue.

In defense of a Church leadership that has nevertheless continued to emphasize ecumenical dialogue, even in the face of too few results to date, however, it must be admitted that the differences which separate Christians from each other are surely never going to be susceptible of any solution if exactly what those differences *are* never get spelled out. Dialogue — that is, serious discussion, hopefully in mutual charity — does provide a means to spell out exactly what those differences are (or perhaps more importantly, as Vatican II itself believed, it helps identify what the areas of *agreement* that might possibly help *unite* Christians actually are).

Among the modern Church leaders committed to ecumenical dialogue, Pope Paul VI was surely in the forefront. During the Second Vatican Council, and just prior to the final debate on the *schema* that became *Unitatis Redintegratio*, on August 6, 1964, Pope Paul VI issued an encyclical entitled *Ecclesiam Suam* on the Paths of the Church in which the pontiff identified as the three most important themes for the Church and the on-going Council the following: Awareness [self-understanding], Renewal, and — *Dialogue*! It was no accident that "dialogue," again, figured up there among the three most important considerations of the day, according to Pope Paul VI. The pope saw the promotion of dialogue as one of the principal aims of the Council. His encyclical thus reflected what we have also noted to have been one of the principal preoccupations of the Council Fathers themselves. At the same time, this emphasis given to the subject by the pope undoubtedly influenced many of the bishops who, in the fall of 1964, when the encyclical appeared, were in the process of debating and approving in its final form the document that would become the Council's Decree on Ecumenism, *Unitatis Redintegratio.*

Pope Paul VI thought that a dialogue between the Church and the modern world was imperative, in particular because, in the Western world at any rate, which had "undergone the profound influence of Christianity," Western secular society had "come to the point of separating and detaching itself from the Christian foundations of its culture" (ES 13). Nonetheless, in the pope's view, dialogue with the world was necessary because, he said, "the Church has something to say. The Church has a message to deliver" (ES 65).

Even more important than dialogue with the world, however, was ecumenical dialogue between and among Christians. Paul VI thought that this ecumenical dialogue had "already begun, and in some areas [was] making real headway." Regarding this ecumenical dialogue, however, he noted that:

> The principle that we are happy to make our own is this: let us stress what we have in common rather than what divides us. This provides a good and fruitful subject for our dialogue. We are ready to carry it out whole-heartedly. We will say more: on many points of difference regarding tradition, spirituality, canon law, and worship, we are ready to study how we can satisfy the legitimate desires of our Christian brothers, still separated from us. It is our dearest wish to embrace them in a perfect union of faith and charity (ES 109).

"Let us stress what we have in common rather than what divides us." Paul VI's optimism here was surely comparable to that of Blessed Pope John XXIII. In the 1960s it was firmly believed, by sincere churchmen at any rate, that dialogue conducted with good will on both sides could accomplish what only miracles up to then had been thought to be able to accomplish. Pope Paul VI quite certainly believed this; he did feel obliged to add, however, that "it is not in our power to compromise with the integrity of the faith or the requirements of charity. We foresee that this will cause misgivings and opposition," he noted, pertinently (*Ibid.*). In particular, he expressed keen regret that the papacy itself was "regarded by many of the separated brethren as being the stumbling block [to unity], because of the primacy of honor and jurisdiction which Christ bestowed upon the Apostle Peter, and which we have inherited from him" (ES 110).

It is interesting that Paul VI spoke here of a "primacy of honor *and* jurisdiction." For the Eastern Orthodox often accord to the bishop of Rome the first of these primacies, that of "honor," while specifically denying to him the second, that of "jurisdiction" — which the First Vatican Council nevertheless did specifically accord to him in a dogmatic canon with anathemas attached. Hence the doctrine of the pope's primacy of jurisdiction is a *defined*, hence an irreformable, doctrine of the Catholic Church. This, in fact, remains the single greatest obstacle and disagreement between the Catholic Church and the Eastern Orthodox Churches.

This idea of the primacy of the successor of Peter in the universal Church as one of the principal obstacles to Christian unity is an idea that we will encounter head on when we very shortly come to look at Pope John Paul II's 1995 encyclical *Ut Unum Sint* on Commitment to Ecumenism. It is perhaps noteworthy, though, that Vatican II's Decree on Ecumenism scarcely touches upon the subject of the primacy, as such, at all. Perhaps this is a serious shortcoming of *Unitatis Redintegratio*. For the primacy of the pope has surely never been anything but that by now famous "elephant in the living room" that somehow nobody wants to mention. Pope Paul VI, for his part, was vividly aware of all this, even as he urged Catholics to press forward with the dialogue that the Council too would shortly after that officially mandate. Pope Paul VI considered the dialogue to be "a principal method of accomplishing the apostolic mission" (ES 81), and he thought that the Council itself would issue "theoretical and practical norms for the guidance of [the] dialogue" (ES 89).

Pope John Paul II, from the beginning of his pontificate, then, also strongly endorsed the idea of dialogue. In his very first encyclical, *Redemptor Hominis* on the Redeemer of Man, issued on March 4, 1979, John Paul II specifically referred back to Paul VI's *Ecclesiam Suam*, and he noted that the self-awareness of the Church, which Paul VI thought was essential for the desired renewal of the faith, was to be formed and developed nowhere else but "in dialogue" (RH 11).

"Dialogue," then, must be considered one of the key ideas animating the Church during and after the Council. In the following sections, we shall have to consider how successful this ecumenical dialogue has been to date (though *whether* it has been completely successful to date does not necessarily invalidate it, either!). But it is nevertheless worth noting here that, prior to Vatican II, dialogue was *not* considered to be a very salient characteristic of the Catholic Church's approach to teaching or missionary endeavor. Proclamation of the Gospel was what counted then, just as Jesus himself, at the beginning of his ministry, declared: "The time is fulfilled, and the kingdom of God is at hand; repent and believe in the Gospel!" (Mk 1:15).

It is, of course, also true, though, that Jesus himself not infrequently engaged in dialogue with various interlocutors, such as the Samaritan woman at the well, or the young man who wanted to know what he must do to inherit eternal life. However, just as often, or more often, Jesus simply proclaimed his teaching in a manner that normally precluded any discussion or debate — that is, any "dialogue." Often Jesus simply threw out his teachings for acceptance or rejection. This is a fact that, in the Gospels, is often if not usually, quite prominent: Jesus simply throws out his teaching, and we are obliged to accept it or reject it (or, sadly, perhaps simply ignore it), as the case may be: "He who has ears to hear, let him hear" (Mt 11:15; Mk 4:9; Lk 8:8).

Historically, the Church too has often issued her teachings and judgments in this take-it-or-leave-it fashion rather than getting too engaged in any such thing as a "dialogue." This was the typical mode, of course, to which Catholics had long become accustomed prior to Vatican II. And in the post-conciliar years, when it became evident that the faith was being watered down in various ways, in spite of the careful specifications and cautions of the Holy See and the bishops, many Catholics almost inevitably came to question the value, and even the validity, of any dialogue: why all this dialogue, they logically asked, if the Church already possesses the truth?

There is actually a great deal to be said for this point of view: the faith *should* be proclaimed "upon the housetops" (Mt 1:27; Lk 12:3) without reservations or apologies, just as the Church has so long been accustomed to do in so many ways. *Since* the faith is true, its cogent and even forceful articulation, like Christ's proclamation of the Kingdom in the Gospels, promotes and encourages *conviction*. Even Pope Paul VI specified that "our dialogue must not weaken our attachment to our faith. In our apostolate, we cannot make vague compromises about the principles of faith and action on which our profession of Christianity is based" (ES 88).

At the same time, however, there is also a place for patient dialogue with those who are not convinced. On appropriate occasions, as we have noted, Jesus himself was prepared to enter into such patient dialogue. In noting the emphasis that both the popes and the Council have now given to it, we can surely see it as an attempt to address a situation in which progress towards Christian unity had come to a virtual standstill: at a minimum, we surely had to start *talking* again! As Winston Churchill is once supposed to have said about diplomacy: "Jaw, jaw, jaw is preferable to war, war, war." The same thing may be true of religious and theological differences as well. Thus, as a result of the initiatives of both pope and Council, the new ecumenism was launched, with results to date that we shall have to look at shortly.

Meanwhile, though, it is worth mentioning here another important factor which has helped bring the subject of dialogue to the fore. This factor is nothing else but the question of *human dignity*. At least in part as a result of the totalitarian excesses of the twentieth century, both Vatican Council II, and, especially, Pope John Paul II, strongly insisted upon this question of human dignity. The recognition and advancement of human dignity was one of the great themes of the Second Vatican Council, in fact; this can be seen most plainly in such conciliar documents as the Council's Pastoral Constitution on the Church in the Modern World, *Gaudium et Spes*, and, especially, its Declaration on Religious Liberty, *Dignitatis Humanae*, which is, quite obviously, *named* "human dignity." But the question of human dignity is also a major concern of *Unitatis Redintegratio* as well.

The human dignity even of those who hold erroneous religious opinions — bluntly, those who subscribe to *false* religions, or who are otherwise in error — requires that they still be *respected as persons*. They may be in error — the Church believes that many of them *are* in error — but they do not forfeit their human dignity thereby. Thus has the Church come to teach and affirm strongly this truth about human dignity — in the face of modern totalitarian regimes only too ready to "liquidate" any who might dare to disagree with the reigning ideology. On a much lower level, today's "political correctness" also aims at eliminating divergent opinions. Honest dialogue, however, must accord respect to human persons as persons, and this therefore provides yet one more reason why Vatican II laid so much stress on dialogue in its pursuit of the new ecumenism.

To this should be added, however, the qualification that none of the official Church documents with which we have been citing here considers dialogue to be anything but a *method*. We quoted Paul VI to that effect above. The substance of the faith is not, and cannot be, altered by engaging in ecumenical dialogue. In approving their Decree on Ecumenism, the Council Fathers took it for granted that this strict adherence to the defined faith would continue to be the case. Moreover, the relevant official Church documents, while encouraging and promoting dialogue, pretty consistently recognize the limitations of dialogue too. The document entitled "Reflections and Suggestions concerning Ecumenical Dialogue" (dated August 15, 1970) issued by the Secretariat for the Promotion of Christian Unity, for example, states the following concerning the *limits* of dialogue:

> Dialogue, however, like all human effort, has its limits. Certain differences between the Churches rest on data of an historical, psychological, and sociological order. They are felt to be still irreducible. Other, deeper ones depend on the way in which one conceives one's own faith and lives it. Dialogue seems powerless here. The participants realize that God is calling them to turn to him in prayer and that he is teaching them to place their confidence in the power of the Holy Spirit alone (VI, 6).

Thus we can affirm, along with the Church, that while dialogue is important and necessary, it is not everything. It is always trumped, for example, and necessarily so, by *truth.*

CHAPTER SIX

CONNECTING WITH THE
ECUMENICAL MOVEMENT

ONCE VATICAN II adopted the new ecumenism as official Church policy, it was probably inevitable that the Catholic Church, owing not merely to her sheer size and numbers, but also to her new and formidable determination, directed from the Holy See, to seek unity with all Christians, would very soon make her a very important if not the dominant factor and presence in the whole ecumenical movement. This, in fact, was precisely what very soon occurred.

An organized ecumenical movement founded under Protestant auspices had been in being since 1910, and had resulted later, in 1948, in the formation of the World Council of Churches (WCC). As we have noted, in accordance with the strictures of Pope Pius XI and some of his predecessors, the Catholic Church took no part whatsoever in this ecumenical movement.

The ecumenical movement itself, though, was nevertheless still going strong at the time of the Second Vatican Council, when one of the more important of the WCC's World Assemblies took place in New Delhi. This was in 1961, the year before Vatican II itself convened. Such, already, was the changed ecumenical climate, however, that, for the first time, Catholic observers were present at this 1961 WCC meeting in New Delhi. The presence of these Catho-

lic observers presaged that of the numerous non-Catholic observers
who would be present at Vatican II.

When, at the Council, *Unitatis Redintegratio* was drawn up
and addressed to those in the ecumenical movement "who invoke
the Triune God and invoke Jesus Christ as Lord and Savior" (UR 1),
some concluded that explicit reference was being made to the 1961
WCC New Delhi Third World Assembly, which had described the
WCC as "a fellowship of Churches which confess the Lord Jesus
Christ as God and Savior according to the Scriptures, and therefore
seek to fulfill together their common calling to the glory of the one
God, Father, Son, and Holy Spirit." Both the WCC and the Catholic
Church were determinedly both Trinitarian and Christocentric, in
other words, and insisted upon defining themselves accordingly.

Nevertheless, in spite of the Catholic Church's original non-
participation, the eventual dominance of this worldwide Church
within the ecumenical movement was almost certainly bound to
come about, if for no other reason than that the sheer numbers of
Catholics among the world's Christians would eventually prevail.
By the end of the twentieth century, Catholics would number more
than one billion adherents worldwide, compared to probably around
220 million members in the Orthodox Churches of the Byzantine-
Slavic traditions, if that many, while, at the same time, there were
also around some 10 million more members to be counted in the
Ancient Churches of the East not in communion with either Rome
or Constantinople. In the Churches and ecclesial communities stemming from the Protestant Reformation, there were perhaps as many
as 180 million at the century's end. Countless others belonging to
evangelical or pentecostal sects added to the total number of Christians in the world, of probably nearly another half billion. However,
the total numbers of Christians in the world along with their affiliations cannot really be calculated with complete exactitude.

Interestingly enough, though, prior to Vatican II, the Byzantine Eastern Orthodox Churches found it possible to participate in
what was then a very heterogeneous ecumenical movement. At the

time, it was conducted under mostly WCC auspices, that is to say, Protestant auspices. Even while keeping their distances from Rome, many Eastern Orthodox Churches nevertheless found it possible to participate as members of the WCC. Given their hierarchy, priesthood, and sacramental system, though, it might have been thought that these Eastern Orthodox Churches would consider themselves closer to the Catholic Church than to communions which had abandoned some or all of these ecclesiastical features — just as the Catholic Church has certainly considered herself closer to *them* from a time well before the issuance of *Unitatis Redintegratio,* as well as since. But such has not actually been the case. Some observers thought (and think) that there is an important sense in which a common "anti-Romanism" has long been a principal factor in linking the member Churches of the WCC together.

Yet another way in which the Eastern Orthodox world resembles the "splintering" of the Protestant world, though, rather than the basic unity of the Catholic Churches in union with the Holy See, is that each of the fifteen or so autonomous Eastern Orthodox Churches is organized along *national* lines — that is, Bulgarian, Greek, Romanian, Russian, Serbian, etc. — whose communicants do not necessarily "mix" (although their Churches are officially in communion with one another).

But communion with the Western Church would evidently be something else again for these Eastern Christians. Evidently the causes and conditions which brought about the original separation between the Eastern and Western Churches have remained too immediate and too painful from the Eastern point of view to allow any such quick or easy reconciliation on their part just because the Catholic Church at Vatican Council II had finally decided to adopt the new ecumenism.

Nevertheless, the adoption of the new ecumenism has proved to be an enormously important factor in the post-conciliar era. Pope Paul VI traveled to Jerusalem for a much publicized meeting with Ecumenical Patriarch Athenagoras I in 1964 while the Council was

still sitting. Pope John Paul II, during his long pontificate, made repeated and extraordinary efforts to court the Orthodox in particular
— while not always finding among them a welcome as warm on the
surface as the welcomes generally accorded by, for example, the Anglicans or the Lutherans who, in both doctrine and discipline (but
not in history or geography!), would seem to be much farther away
from the Catholic Church than the Eastern Orthodox.

What quickly became manifest once Catholic ecumenical
efforts got underway in the post-conciliar era, however, was that
these efforts by the Church were henceforth soon to be found pretty
much driving the whole ecumenical movement. It is only necessary
to consult the section entitled "Ecumenism and Interreligious Dialogue" in the latest *Catholic Almanac* in order to verify this in terms
of the various "bilateral commissions" meeting or the most recent
"agreed statements" concluded. Following Vatican II and the Decree on Ecumenism, in fact, the Catholic Church more or less *took
over the leadership* of the ecumenical movement. If this is perhaps
an exaggeration, it is not one by much. Moreover, Catholic dominance of the ecumenical movement proved not to be based so much
on the Church's sheer numbers of adherents alone, although that
was surely a factor, as upon the sheer determination and efficiency
with which the Catholic Church in the post-conciliar era began to
"organize" the ecumenical dialogue on all sides, regularly setting
up theological commissions and organizing such things as conferences and colloquia, for example, in order to carry on the desired
ecumenical dialogues.

During the course of the post-conciliar era, these theological
commissions, under that name or some variant name such as "collo-
quium," "dialogue," or "conversation," have been set up between the
Pontifical Council for Promoting Christian Unity (which eventually
succeeded Cardinal Augustin Bea's Secretariat for the Promotion
of Christian Unity set up at Vatican II), and practically every other
possible organized Christian communion or grouping in the world.
There are today such commissions continuing to carry on consulta-

tions between Catholics and Anglicans, the Assyrian Church of the East, Baptists, Disciples of Christ, Evangelicals, Lutherans, Orthodox in both the Byzantine Greek and Slavic traditions, Pentecostals, and Reformed. There have similarly been operating commissions (recently combined into one) with some of the Ancient Eastern Churches: the Armenian Orthodox, the Assyrian Church of the East, the Coptic Orthodox, the Malankara Orthodox, the Syrian, and the Malankara Jacobite Syrian Orthodox Churches.

Some of these theological commissions have made greater progress than others. In some cases, major and indeed unprecedented agreed statements have been produced. And beyond all of this effort, additional dialogue has also been carried on even where no actual joint theological commission exists.

More publicized than the work of these joint ecumenical theological commissions, however, have been the meetings of the popes with the heads of other Churches and communions. Not infrequently, these meetings have resulted in joint or common declarations setting forth areas of doctrinal or theological agreement previously unheard of or even imagined. One of the more dramatic of these meetings, of course, occurred even before the end of Vatican II. This was the meeting already mentioned between Pope Paul VI and Ecumenical Patriarch Athenagoras I of Constantinople, which took place in the course of a joint pilgrimage to the Holy Land by both prelates in January, 1964. This pilgrimage was conducted before the watching eyes of virtually the whole world, garnering extensive and dramatic media coverage. It inaugurated a whole series of meetings between the pope and patriarch which would come to characterize the improved relations between the Catholic Church and the Eastern Orthodox Churches in the post-conciliar era. These meetings show no signs of diminishing. Rather the contrary: they have become an expected and regular feature of the religious and Christian scene today.

CHAPTER SEVEN

RELATIONS WITH
THE EASTERN ORTHODOX

THE 1964 MEETING IN Jerusalem between Pope Paul VI and Ecumenical Patriarch Athenagoras I proved to be the beginning of the further extensive contacts between the two Churches that would take place in the forty-plus years following the adoption of the new ecumenism by the Catholic Church at Vatican Council II. The whole affair went extremely well, as it happened, featuring a joint recitation of the "Our Father" in both Latin and Greek and an exchange of gifts — Pope Paul VI gave the patriarch a gold chalice symbolic of the Eucharist, considered perhaps the most important common essential element of the faith shared by both Churches; and the patriarch presented the pope with the kind of pectoral chain worn by Orthodox bishops symbolic of their apostolic succession — a gift which certainly underlined the patriarch's recognition that the pope *was* a bishop (of Rome) validly ordained in the apostolic succession.

As a direct result of their meeting in Jerusalem in 1964, Pope Paul VI, and the Orthodox Ecumenical Patriarch Athenagoras I, came to issue, on December 7, 1965, the day before the end of Vatican Council II, the first of their Common Declarations officially lifting the joint excommunications which had been issued against pope and patriarch by another patriarch and a papal legate back in the year 1054. The lifting of these joint excommunications was a symbolic action only, since, strictly speaking, the original mutual excommunications, although long considered to have inaugurated the formal schism between East and West, were actually personal and did not strictly apply to the successors of the patriarch and the pope of the day.

In their first Common Declaration, however, the two prelates from the East and the West, mutually declared their hopes for a restoration of "full communion of faith, brotherly concord, and sacramental life." Their joint statement was dramatically read out before the Council Fathers at Vatican II by the newly ordained Dutch Bishop Johannes Willebrands, who in the coming years would be a key ecumenical figure on the Catholic side. The statement emphasized that the two prelates, Catholic and Orthodox, would omit nothing "which charity might inspire and which might facilitate the relations" between the Churches of Rome and Constantinople. The ecumenical patriarch had the same statement publicly read out in Istanbul.

In another Common Declaration two years later, on October 27, 1967, the same pope and patriarch emphasized their joint conviction "that the restoration of full communion [was] to be found within the framework of the renewal of the Church and of Christians in fidelity to the traditions of the Fathers and to the inspirations of the Holy Spirit, who remains always with the Church." This new spirit of concord between the earthly head of the Catholic Church and the spiritual head of the Eastern Orthodox Churches, which would continue in the post-conciliar years, was thus a direct result of the renewal of the Church undertaken by Vatican Council II. Forty years later, Patriarch Bartholomew I of Constantinople celebrated in Rome with Pope John Paul II the anniversary of the historic meeting of their predecessors in Jerusalem, and in a joint statement the pope and patriarch vowed to continue "the journey we have undertaken towards full communion in Christ," even while recognizing "certain problems and misunderstandings" that had recently impeded progress.

It was never really very likely, of course, that the opening of the lines of communication between the pope and the ecumenical patriarch that have continued since 1964 could have resulted in any *immediate* prospect of actual reunion after nearly nine hundred years of formal ecclesiastical separation. This indeed proved to be the case. For one thing, the ecumenical patriarch is not the head of a single communion, as is the pope. The ecumenical patriarch is, rather, only the *primus inter pares*, the first among equals, of the heads of some fifteen different national Byzantine and Slavic Orthodox Churches. Although they are all in communion with each other, some of these national Orthodox Churches — those of Alexandria, Antioch, Jerusalem, Moscow, Serbia, Romania, Bulgaria, and Georgia — all have their own patriarchs. Other independent Orthodox Churches are similarly headed by their own archbishops or metropolitans. According to Orthodox doctrine, these independent, autocephalous (single-headed) Churches in communion with each other constitute the principal model for the Church of Christ, as it has come down from the apostles.

The Catholic doctrine, of course, is that all these national or independent Churches, while indeed they should enjoy autonomy as well as doctrinal and sacramental communion with each other, should nevertheless also be in communion with, and under, the successor of the head apostle, Peter, the bishop of Rome, the pope. The Orthodox model of the true Church, in the Catholic view, fails to reflect the apostolic Church completely in that it lacks, precisely, any successor of the head apostle, Peter. The original apostles formed a college headed by Peter; their successors, the bishops, need to be united with the successor of Peter, the bishop of Rome.

Pope John Paul II, in some of his important visits, tried to take this message of the necessity of union with the successor of Peter to some of the individual Orthodox Churches he visited. In this particular effort, he received more encouragement in some of the places he visited (Romania) than in some others (Georgia, Sinai). As a result of the Polish pope's efforts, however, there did not yet seem

to be any wide recognition on the part of the Orthodox Churches
that their claim to have handed down intact and without change the
beliefs and practices of the apostolic Church *was* in any way lacking
in one of the most crucial and characteristic features of the Church
as described in the New Testament, namely, the fact that the original apostles (who would be succeeded by the bishops, as both the
Catholic and the Orthodox Churches hold and teach) *were,* in fact,
headed in a unique way by one among them, Peter.

However, in spite of the fact that the continuing contacts between the Catholic Church and the Orthodox Churches have already
in many respects now "broken the mould," and that the relationships
between them have now probably been changed forever as a result,
the fact remains that ecclesiastical unity between them has nevertheless not been achieved. It has not been achieved, in an important
sense it must be said, because of the continuing inability or unwillingness of the Eastern Orthodox to recognize the primacy of Peter
over the whole Church. The lines of communication between the
Catholic and Orthodox Churches have remained open in the post-
conciliar era on many, if not on most, issues; actual reunion, however, has not as yet come about because there is not yet a fundamental
agreement about the nature of the Church.

Oddly enough, in spite of all the dialogue, the Joint International Commission for Theological Dialogue between the Orthodox
Church and the Catholic Church, up to the death of Pope John Paul
II, had not yet initiated any formal discussions on the question of
the primacy of the Church of Rome itself: thus, the elephant in the
living room continued to be ignored.

Nevertheless, the custom has now apparently become permanent of sending Roman delegations to Istanbul on the Feast of the
patron saint of the Church of Constantinople, Saint Andrew, on November 30 of each year, and of receiving Greek delegations in Rome
on the Feast of Saints Peter and Paul on June 29 of each year. On
this latter date, in 2004, the Ecumenical Patriarch Bartholomew I
visited Rome, where he participated in a Eucharistic liturgy presid-

ed over by Pope John Paul II. The program followed those observed during the previous visits of the Patriarch Dimitrios (1987) and that of Bartholomew himself (1995). This included full participation in the Liturgy of the Word, a joint proclamation by the pope and the patriarch of the Niceno-Constantinopolitan Creed in Greek, and a final blessing imparted by both prelates. And in a Common Declaration released on July 1, 2004, the two prelates said that:

> Our meeting in Rome today also enables us to face certain problems and misunderstandings that have recently surfaced. The long experience of the "dialogue of charity" comes to our aid precisely in these circumstances, so that difficulties can be faced serenely without slowing or clouding our progress on the journey we have undertaken towards full communion in Christ.

During the patriarch's visit, he asked the pope to return relics reposing in St. Peter's of two great Eastern saints, predecessors of his in the See of Constantinople, St. Gregory Nazianzus (330-390) and St. John Chrysostom (349-407). The relics of St. Gregory had been brought to Rome in the eighth century by some Byzantine nuns in order to save them from the ravages of iconoclasm, then going on in the East, while those of St. John had been brought to Rome during the time of the Crusades. Pope John Paul II agreed to return some of these relics. A ceremony for their veneration in St. Peter's was organized for November 27, 2004. This brought Patriarch Bartholomew back to Rome for his second visit during 2004. At the ceremony passages from the writings of the two holy Greek Fathers were read at a Liturgy of the Word. That same day, a Catholic delegation led by the president of the Pontifical Council for Promoting Christian Unity, Cardinal Walter Kasper, accompanied Bartholomew back to Istanbul with the relics. There, on the Feast of St. Andrew, November 30, the relics were transferred to the Orthodox enclave in Istanbul, the Phanar, and placed in the patriarchal Church of St. George.

Patriarch Bartholomew said that he considered this event "the most important one in my patriarchal service.... I am deeply moved and very happy. Not only I, personally, but also the whole of the Church of Constantinople, and, I can say without reserve, the whole of Orthodoxy." Thus did the ecumenical dialogue with Eastern Orthodoxy go on. At the conclusion of this book, we shall look at the meetings that took place in Istanbul on the feast of St. Andrew in 2007 with the ecumenical patriarch and Pope Benedict XVI and at Rome in 2008 when the patriarch was again present at the liturgy for the commemoration of St. Peter and St. Paul on June 29, 2008. On this last date, the ecumenical patriarch participated in a service promulgating a Pauline Year — a year commemorating the 2000th anniversary of the birth of the great Apostle to the Gentiles.

Always in the same optimistic vein, the bilateral joint Catholic-Orthodox International Commission for Theological Dialogue established as far back as 1979 worked steadily through the whole post-conciliar era on a number of agreed statements indicating specific agreement between Catholics and Orthodox on a number of subjects, such as "The Mystery of the Church and the Eucharist," "The Sacrament of Order," and "Uniatism" — this last subject being a particularly difficult subject in the Orthodox view, and one which caused the interruption of regular meetings of the Commission at its meeting held in Baltimore in 2000. Only five years later, in June, 2005, with the visit of the Metropolitan Ioannis Zizioulas of Pergamon, representing Patriarch Bartholomew I at the annual joint celebration of the Feast of Saints Peter and Paul, was it announced that all fourteen Orthodox Churches had now re-named representatives to the Catholic-Orthodox International Commission; and that the stalled dialogue would resume in line with the express wish of the new Pope Benedict XVI.

As a result, the ecumenical talks between the Catholics and Eastern Orthodox were indeed resumed in 2006. These resumed talks might even now, finally, include talks on subject of the primacy, it was stated. However, the kind of final agreement that might eventually make reunion possible still seemed distant in spite of the undeniable progress.

In considering whether any real progress towards ultimate unity has nevertheless been made, though, it is important to realize how far the two Churches have actually come. Particularly where the Eastern Orthodox are concerned, it is not easy to change the outlook or habits of centuries (anymore than it is easy to do so in the West). In an address delivered at Georgetown University in the fall of 1997, the same Ecumenical Patriarch Bartholomew I, who was so happy at the return of the relics that had been bought out, nevertheless on that earlier occasion had correctly pointed out that between Catholics and the Orthodox "the manner in which we exist has become *ontologically different*" — meaning, no doubt, wholly different ways of thinking and acting. The patriarch added, though, that "no one ignores the fact that the model for all of us is the *Theanthropos* (God-man) Jesus Christ. But which model? No one ignores that the incorporation in him is achieved within his body, the Church. But whose Church?"

The way forward, according to Patriarch Bartholomew I, would require not only further dialogue in order to achieve greater mutual understanding; it would also require further lived experience in common while thinking and acting in new modes. Even as he underlined the difficulty in all of this, the patriarch nevertheless declared that "our heart requires that we seek again our common foundations and the original starting point that we share so that, retrospectively, we can discover the point and the reasons for our divergence that led to separate courses, and be able, by lifting blame, to proceed thereafter on the same road...."

Obviously, the ecumenical patriarch represents thinking among the Orthodox that coincides with the kind of thinking among Catholics that led to the new ecumenism at Vatican II. Yet in pursuing his course, the patriarch too regularly encountered not a few obstacles within his own Churches that indicate that the way forward may still be far from smooth. Getting all fifteen or so autocephalous

Orthodox Churches to name representatives to the joint Catholic-Orthodox International Commission to take part in the continuing theological dialogue apparently took some doing. And in February, 2003, for example, the same Patriarch Bartholomew had found it necessary to declare in schism a group of Greek monks on Mount Athos who had withdrawn their obedience to him because he was even willing to dialogue with Catholics! Considering Pope John Paul II a "heretic," these monks had draped their monastery with black flags and banners reading "Orthodoxy or Death"!

Thus, the current and now virtually regularized ecumenical contacts between Catholics and Orthodox — including especially the regular contacts between the pope and the ecumenical patriarch — have continued and will very likely continue still. But even with the best will in the world, these contacts will still encounter difficulties. At the same time, though, Pope John Paul II, during his pontificate, scarcely limited his contacts with the Eastern Orthodox to the ecumenical patriarch of Constantinople. Of course, he continued to show great and continuing respect for the latter, having issued no less than four Common Declarations (the latest as recently as June, 2004) jointly with Patriarchs Dimitrios I and Bartholomew I. In addition, though, the pope also took his message concerning the need for Christian unity separately to other individual countries where Orthodoxy is the prevailing faith. In some of these countries, he occasionally encountered outright hostility, but the Polish pope persisted nonetheless.

In one country where Orthodox hostility to the Catholic Church has been substantial, namely, Greece, the pope nevertheless managed to make a visit there in May, 2001, and he issued an extensive and unprecedented Common Statement along with Christodoulos, the archbishop of Athens and all Greece, while "standing before the bema of the Areopagus, from which Saint Paul, the great Apostle to the Nations... preached to the Athenians the One true God, Father, Son, and Holy Spirit...." The two bishops, of Athens and of Rome respectively, reaffirmed their desire for Christian unity, affirmed the need for human dignity in the modern world, deplored war and violence, questioned globalization, and praised the prospects for European union. This was just one more instance of the efforts in which Pope John Paul II proved himself indefatigable, particularly where the Eastern Orthodox were concerned.

One of John Paul II's great ambitions, often mentioned by him, was to pay an official visit to Russia on invitation from the Russian Orthodox patriarch of Moscow. This goal eluded him, however. It eluded him not only because of long-standing differences over such items as the restitution of Catholic Church property turned over to the Orthodox by Josef Stalin when the latter outlawed the Catholic Church; but, in particular, because in February, 2002, wishing to regularize the status of Catholics in Russia, the Catholic Church elevated the four Catholic "apostolic administrations" that existed in the country to the status of regular Catholic dioceses. The patriarch of Moscow interpreted this purely administrative move as an attempt on the part of the Catholic Church to promote what was called Catholic "proselytism" in territory that traditionally "belonged" to the Russian Orthodox Church. As a result of his suspicions of what he called Catholic proselytism, the patriarch rejected any further direct contact with the pope.

This was not the first time that the Catholic Church had been accused of proselytism by Moscow. Indeed, it was an accusation not entirely unheard of among some other Orthodox leaders. One of the factors that lent credence to the accusation in Russia at this time was apparently the fact that, after seventy-five years of Communist rule, including regular efforts carried out by the Communist government to stamp out religion and promote atheism, Russia had become extensively de-Christianized in many respects. Although the country certainly remained the home "territory" of the Russian Orthodox Church, many Russians nevertheless remained unbaptized and were not active members or communicants of any Church at all. In the new post-Communist climate of "freedom" (relatively speaking), however, some new converts to Christianity there turned directly to the Catholic Church requesting baptism. This, according to the Russian patriarch, was "Catholic proselytism."

Now the Catholic Church is not going to refuse baptism and the other sacraments to anyone professing belief in her teaching and prepared to submit to her discipline who requests such sacraments. She is placed in the world, precisely, to offer the Word of God and the means of sanctification and salvation to sinners, and she is surely not going to turn any such sinners away for "political" reasons or merely in order to get along better with, say, the Russian Orthodox Church. This is hardly the same thing as "proselytism" (or "sheep stealing") on the territory of the Russian Orthodox Church. Yet it is at least understandable that the patriarch of Moscow might see these things somewhat differently.

Many of the Catholics living in Russia today, moreover, are there because of earlier mass deportations from their original homelands by successive Russian or Soviet governments. These Catholics are Poles, Lithuanians, and such. The deportations of them were carried out both by the Czars and by the Communists in the earlier Czarist, and the later Soviet, empires. The Catholic Church, however, has been legally recognized in Russia since at least 1783. There is no reason at all why she should not have a regularly organized diocesan and parish structure there to serve those Catholics whose permanent home is now in Russia. The Church's action in setting up four dioceses extending across the immense territory of this huge country in no way implied any Catholic plan or desire to "proselytize" or to somehow try to "supplant" the Russian Orthodox Church in Russia.

Thus, the Russian Orthodox Church still has much to learn, apparently — and might well look to the ecumenical patriarchs of Constantinople as a model in this regard — about how Churches are really obliged to operate today in the conditions of a *diaspora* or "dispersion" of Christians and of Christian Churches throughout many parts of today's globalized world. For example, the Russian Orthodox Church is without any question legally allowed to operate her own Churches and serve her own faithful in North America — not exactly her traditional "territory." So should not the Catholic Church be allowed to do the same in ministering to her faithful in Russia? In the meantime, this very same "national" Russian Orthodox Church evidently has much to *un*learn with regard to the dangers of relying upon the power of the state to try to maintain Christianity. At the present time the civil law in Russia greatly hampers the freedom of non-Orthodox bodies in Russia — to the apparent satisfaction of the Russian Orthodox Church, at least at the moment. But no Christian Church should be trying any longer to rely upon governments to maintain their positions in a given country or society.

It has also been reliably reported in the West that the same Patriarch Alexei II of Moscow who so regularly rebuffed Pope John Paul II is himself a former KGB agent! — as is the Russian President (and later premier), Vladimir Putin, for that matter. In the light of such factors as these, it seems likely that the kind of reconciliation between the Catholic Church and the Russian Orthodox Church which Pope John Paul II always so ardently hoped to see will surely have to come about under another patriarch and another pope.

The Catholic Church, for her part, squarely tried to face, and precisely at Vatican II, the issues of what ought to be today the relationships between Church and state, as well as those between the various Christian bodies and denominations now co-existing upon the same territories. As increased ecumenical contacts continue, it is to be hoped that greater mutual understanding, as well as continuing, if not enhanced, peaceful relations, will prevail among the various Christian Churches and communions. These Churches are still obliged, after all, to try to live peacefully in the same world together, even as they attempt to sort out and hopefully resolve their own disagreements with each other.

CHAPTER EIGHT

THE ANCIENT CHURCHES OF THE EAST

THE HAPPY CONDITION of formerly somewhat hostile separated Christian Churches now interacting together in various ways and, at the very least, maintaining relatively cordial relations with each other, has been steadily developing in the post-conciliar era, not only in the case of some of the Churches in the Byzantine or Slavic Orthodox traditions, as we have observed in the previous chapter; but also with respect to those Ancient Eastern Churches that are not in communion with either Constantinople or Rome. These ancient communions became separated from the main Christian body as a result of breaks which followed the ancient Councils of Ephesus (431 A.D.) and Chalcedon (451 A.D.).

These Ancient Churches of the East include, first of all, the Christian body which broke away from the universal Church following the Council of Ephesus. This body is today known as the Assyrian Church of the East. Formerly, it was often known as the Nestorian Church, although this latter designation fails to do justice to the extremely checkered history of this ancient communion, a history which includes a number of reunions and separations over the centuries.

As for the Ancient Churches which broke away after the Council of Chalcedon, they are included in the listing that follows. They themselves are sometimes referred to as "Orthodox" — but in the case of these ancient communions, the word "Orthodox" does not mean exactly the same thing as it does when applied to the Eastern Orthodox Churches in the Byzantine and Slavic traditions; for these ancient communions are *not* in communion with the various national Eastern Orthodox Churches and the patriarch of Constantinople, any more than they are in communion with the Western Church and the bishop of Rome, either. They got separated in antiquity. These Ancient Churches of the East that are included in this category are: the Armenian Apostolic Church, the Coptic Orthodox Church of Egypt, the Ethiopian Orthodox Church and that of Eritrea, the Syrian Orthodox Church (often called "Jacobite") and the Malankara Syrian Orthodox Church of India. These latter six communions have historically been considered "Monophysite" — referring to the idea of "one nature" in Christ, as opposed to the two natures, divine and human, specified by the Council of Chalcedon as actually existing in Christ.

Now Monophysitism, as historically formulated and described, is very definitely a heresy, and any continuing insistence in holding to it on the part of any of these communions would naturally preclude any reunion with them on the part of the Catholic Church. However, there is today some question about how rigidly or consistently some of these ancient communions really did adhere to, or still adhere to, the historic heresy that has been defined and condemned as Monophysitism.

As far back as 1951, in his encyclical *Sempiternus Rex* on the 15th Centenary of the Council of Chalcedon, Pope Pius XII suggested that the ancient separation may have been based more on a misunderstanding of the doctrine of Chalcedon than upon an outright rejection of it. Pope Pius XII thought that these separated Churches perhaps erred "mainly in their use of words in defining the doctrine of the Incarnation. This may be demonstrated from their liturgical and theological books" (SR 26). The pontiff added that "today we are accustomed to retrace and weigh the events of bygone ages more calmly than in the past" (SR 40).

Of course in 1951, Pope Pius XII was still thinking in terms of a simple "return" of these communions to Catholic orthodoxy and obedience. Nevertheless, he certainly anticipated Vatican II in believing that future "research" (carried out without "jealousy or anger"), along with serious dialogue, might possibly open up a path to reunion with one or more of these Ancient Eastern Churches. Following the Council and the issuance of *Unitatis Redintegratio*, the popes have pursued ecumenical contacts with them with special application, sensitivity, and zeal. Even though the numbers of their faithful are not great on a worldwide scale — many of them have lived and survived for centuries under Muslim or other non-Christian rule — it would nevertheless be of enormous ecumenical significance if one or more of these ancient Churches were to accept reunion with the Catholic Church and enter into communion with the successor of Peter — under conditions allowing them to maintain their historical rites and practices, as these things are understood today.

Although the Eastern Catholic Churches already in communion with the See of Rome — covered in a separate Vatican II document of their own, *Orientalium Ecclesiarum* — form an integral part of the Catholic Church (which is thus *not* just "the Roman Catholic Church," as we have already noted), the addition of one or more of these Ancient Eastern Churches as a result of the new post-Vatican II ecumenism could have simply enormous significance for the future of the restoration of Christian unity generally. It would mean that separated Christian Churches *do not have to remain separated* — that historic separations do not have to be *permanent* and *irrevocable*!

The Holy See has long been very aware of the potential here. In the early 1970s, Pope Paul VI gave almost as much attention to receiving a number of these Ancient Eastern Church leaders as he did to his much more widely publicized contacts with Anglican and Eastern Orthodox leaders. Following his election to the papacy, Pope John Paul II took up where his predecessor had left off, and, from 1984 on, he received a number of the Ancient Eastern prel-

ates. He also issued with them jointly a number of agreed Common
Declarations of faith. These efforts of his became intensified as the
Third Millennium of Christianity approached. John Paul II evidently hoped that all his efforts, whether with the Byzantine-Slavic
Orthodox, or with the Ancient Eastern Churches, would achieve
some tangible ecumenical success to be celebrated along with the
millennial commemorations. This was not to be, as things turned
out, but this was surely not because of any lack of efforts on John
Paul's part.

In particular, John Paul II's meetings with Karekin II, Catholicos of all the Armenians, in Rome in November, 2000, and in Armenia in September, 2001, seemed to bring possible reunion tan-
talizingly closer, at least in words; the two Churchmen seemed to
be so near to one another, in fact, that one might seriously and legitimately have been moved to ask why, indeed, *was* there still any
separation?

Yet the same question persisted when the same Armenian
Catholicos and patriarch visited Rome again in May, 2008, and met
with Pope Benedict XVI. Doctrinally, there did not seem to be any
significant differences between the Roman and the Armenian head
bishops. Nevertheless, actual unity between the Church of Rome
and the Armenian Orthodox Church was not proclaimed explicitly,
although good will was mutually stated and observed on both sides,
as had become the custom. Actual unity, however, would evidently
have to await further developments and an explicit statement by the
competent Church authorities.

And it was still the case, of course, that in February, 2003,
representatives from all six of the Ancient Eastern Churches that
had become separated from the main body of Christianity following
the Council of Chalcedon met in Rome to establish a single Joint
Commission for Theological Dialogue with the Catholic Church.
Henceforth ecumenical dialogue with these Churches would proceed through this one Joint Commission. Its formation indicated a
recognition by these ancient communions both that a commonality

of faith certainly existed, and that reunion was possible. Pope John Paul II reminded the representatives of the Churches present that "substantial ecumenical progress has already been made between the Catholic Church and the different Oriental Orthodox Churches. Essential clarifications have been reached with regard to traditional controversies about Christology, and this has enabled us to profess together the faith we hold in common." In January, 2004, representatives of these ancient Churches of the East, as well as observers from the Holy See, met again, this time in Cairo, Egypt, although no further new ground was apparently broken on this latter occasion.

As for the Assyrian Church of the East, which became separated from the universal Church following the Council of Ephesus in 431, an extensive Common Declaration was issued by Pope John Paul II and His Holiness Mar Dinkha IV, Catholicos-Patriarch of the Assyrian Church of the East, on November 11, 1994. In this historic Common Declaration, both Churches acknowledged that, in spite of differences stretching over many centuries, both Churches still professed the same faith handed down from the apostles in a real union of both divine and human natures in the one divine person of Jesus Christ. In this statement, in effect, the Christological definition of the Council of Chalcedon was repeated almost verbatim. It would thus seem that the Christological question — which was ostensibly the reason for the original separation — had effectively been resolved. Five of the seven sacraments were mentioned and affirmed. The two Churches agreed to recognize each other as "Sister Churches" — although full communion, as such, was again not restored.

Not only that, but on July 20, 2001, the Pontifical Council for Promoting Christian Unity issued a set of "Guidelines for Admission to the Eucharist between the Chaldean [Catholic] Church and the Assyrian Church of the East." In view of the difficult situations of both of these Eastern Churches, not only in the primary home country of both, namely, war-torn Iraq, but also in the diasporas of both — but also in view of the fact that no differences between the

Christological and Eucharistic faiths of the two Churches could any longer be discerned — it was decided that intercommunion *could be permitted* between this former Nestorian Church and the Chaldean Catholic Church. The Chaldean Catholic Church, in 1553, had broken away from the Nestorian Church, as it was then called, and had sought and achieved reunion with the Holy See; it became a bona fide Eastern Catholic Church. However, both the Catholic and the non-Catholic communions in this tradition were the descendants of this ancient "Nestorian Church" — a term which, however, as we have noted, does not entirely accurately describe the complexity of the ecclesiastical history involved. In the event, though, intercommunion between the two bodies came to be approved.

Nevertheless, the agreement on intercommunion between the Chaldean Catholic Church and the Assyrian Church of the East was not the first instance of intercommunion in the post-Vatican II period. Intercommunion is permitted by the Catholic Church's rules in some other very limited cases with the Eastern Orthodox, in particular, in some cases where their own clergy are not available, either to the Catholic or to the Orthodox communicants. But this new, now permitted intercommunion between the Chaldean Catholic Church and the Assyrian Church of the East nevertheless amounted to a very real step towards final full reunion. It was one of the most significant developments since the new post-Vatican II ecumenism began, and it came about as a result of the systematic pursuit of the kind of ecumenical dialogue which Vatican II had called for and mandated.

It was significant too in that the Holy See only allowed this intercommunion after carefully studying and finally approving the validity of the very ancient Anaphora of Addai and Mari, as it is called — a rite for the celebration of the Eucharist employed since apostolic times in the Assyrian Church of the East. Yet it is a rite which lacks an explicit Institution Narrative (e.g., from Eucharistic Prayer III in the Roman rite, "On the night he was betrayed, he took bread and gave you thanks and praise. He broke the bread, gave it to his disciples, and said: Take this, all of you, and eat it: This is my body which will be given up for you.").

The Catholic Church has normally considered a proper Institution Narrative to be an essential and constitutive element of any valid Eucharistic celebration. After extensive study, however, it was finally decided in the case of the Anaphora of Addai and Mari that an Institution Narrative is *equivalently present*. The rite goes back to the very beginnings of the Church; it was always intended to be, and was always celebrated as, a true Eucharist in continuity with the Last Supper of the Lord Jesus Christ. On these grounds, the Holy See finally decided to accept its validity, restoring thereby another chapter to the long history of the variety of spiritual riches found in the Church established by Christ.

In all of this, we have been able to look here only at a few of the highlights of the post-conciliar relationships between the Catholic Church and the Eastern Churches, both those in the Byzantine-Slavic Orthodox tradition, and those we now know as and call the Ancient Churches of the East. There is much more that we could have said, but the highlights we have covered will have to suffice. All in all, in spite of slow progress and a number of disappointments, it does have to be conceded that the new ecumenism launched by Vatican II *has* created a new ecumenical situation for us vis-à-vis the Eastern Churches — a new situation that at the very least allows us to think that reunion with them is indeed possible — and, in some degree, that such a reunion could perhaps even come about sooner than we might think.

CHAPTER NINE

TRADITIONS IN TRANSITION

I F REUNION WITH SOME of the Eastern Churches is now at least imaginable as a result of all the ecumenical efforts exerted in the post-conciliar era, it remains harder to imagine how real reunion might be possible between the Catholic Church and those Churches and ecclesial communions stemming from the Protestant Reformation. In a way, this is paradoxical because, at least in some respects, Catholics have more in common with our Protestant brethren than with our Eastern brethren: we have in common with them a shared history and geography, similar views on Church and state, a certain dynamism with respect to the secular world generally, and a pronounced missionary thrust — among other similarities.

In the case of our Eastern brethren, however, even though they have substantially preserved both doctrinal orthodoxy and the sacramental system, we have nevertheless become in many respects, as Ecumenical Patriarch Bartholomew I so aptly expressed it, "ontologically different." Catholics and Protestants instead in some ways remain "ontologically the same," in spite of differences in doctrine and discipline.

It is true that the history of Christianity in the East has been quite different from its history in the West. For one thing, most of the Churches of the East have had to live for centuries under alien and usually oppressive governments, often Muslim; the chief concern of some of these communions has often been how to survive at all, let alone flourish, under such regimes as the Persian or Ottoman Empires — or the Soviet Empire later on in modern times! And even where the regimes or governments in the Eastern sphere were themselves Christian, they still tended to be authoritarian governments if not despotisms that often ruled their "national" Orthodox Churches with an iron hand. There was hardly any such concept at all in those parts of the world as "the separation of Church and state"; the state ruled; the Church was subordinate; that was that. Russian Czar Peter the Great, for instance, actually *abolished* the Moscow patriarchate and ruled the Russian Orthodox Church himself directly through a synod which he appointed.

But as Cardinal Walter Kasper has pointed out in his 2004 book *That They May All Be One*, these Eastern Churches "are now free for the first time — free from the Byzantine emperors, free from the Ottomans, free from the Czars, and free from the totalitarian Communist system; but they see themselves facing an entirely transformed world in which they must find their way." Cardinal Kasper goes on to say, one would imagine, quite correctly that: "This will take time and require patience."

But up to now the Churches of the East have thus mostly not known the relative freedom and independence of the Churches in the West, whether Catholic or Protestant — although, needless to say, the struggle for the Churches in the West to remain free from the state control of absolute monarchs or revolutionary governments has also been constant right up until the present day. The conditions under which the Eastern Churches generally had to live, though, were bound, almost by themselves, to discourage, say, the kind of missionary impulse which has been so marked a characteristic of the Catholic Church, as well as of some of the Protestant communions.

Given the kind of situations in which they generally found themselves, the Eastern Churches were by and large obliged to hunker down, so to speak; and what most of them proved to be good at was preserving their own traditions, liturgical and otherwise: what had been handed down was sacrosanct. Change or "development," on the other hand, was sometimes hard to come by. In one very important sense, of course, this tenacious adherence to tradition at all costs is an essential characteristic of any authentic Christianity. After all, a religion based on the words and acts of Jesus Christ faithfully preserved and handed down in the Church which he himself established upon the apostles has surely been obliged to be "conservative" about not a few things. Pope Paul VI once observed that the Catholic Church had to be what he styled "tenaciously conservative" if she was to succeed in preserving and handing on what was essential; she obviously could not deviate or compromise where essentials were concerned. The pope's words in this regard came in a speech of his delivered in Uganda during his visit there in 1969; speaking about the Church in Africa to Africans, he said:

> You know that the Church is particularly tenacious, we may even say conservative.... To make sure that the message of revealed doctrine cannot be altered, the Church has ever set down her treasure of truth in certain concepts and verbal formulas. Even when these formulas are difficult, at times, she obliges us to preserve them textually. We are not the inventors of faith, we are its custodians.

According to the liberal Vaticanologist, the late Peter Hebblethwaite, a biographer of Pope Paul VI, this was the only time that Pope Paul VI ever used the word "conservative" in one of his speeches or allocutions. But he was, of course, absolutely correct that the Church is innately and necessarily conservative where anything touching upon doctrine or the deposit of the faith is concerned. Still, this in no way means that the Church is obliged to be hidebound, reactionary, or *immobiliste*; there can still be both "development of doctrine" *and* development of Church rites, practices, and even structures.

In the West, the Catholic Church, especially the papacy, managed to maintain down through history a measure of freedom and independence from the stifling embrace that even professedly "Christian" governments were so often tempted to employ (not to speak of those that were openly hostile to the Church!). This relative freedom and independence of the Catholic Church thus enabled her to address problems with which she was faced not just by simply standing pat on tradition.

New problems sometimes required new solutions. This was one of the reasons why a "living Church" was required in the first place. It has never been possible always just to go "by the book." That was one of the capital mistakes of the Protestant Reformation — even when the book in question was the Holy Bible! The world of today is very different from the world of the Roman Empire into which the Church of Christ first came to birth — and it is very different from the medieval society during which the Catholic Church in the West was dominant. Adaptation and development have always been necessary. Tradition, though always both essential and indispensable, could never be completely sufficient.

Upon reflection it is hard to credit, for example, that the supreme living magisterium, or teaching authority, with which Christ endowed his Church, could simply have somehow become suspended indefinitely following the Second Council of Nicaea in 787 A.D. Yet that is what the doctrine of the Orthodox Church to the effect that only the first seven of the Church's ecumenical councils are valid would pretty much seem to amount to in the end. According to this view of things, Christ's Church apparently no longer has the authority she possessed in the early centuries to teach "all nations" (Mt 28:19; 13:10; Lk 24:47) with the voice of Christ himself.

When the Orthodox object, for example, to the *Filioque* clause that Pope Benedict VIII added to the Nicene Creed in 1014 — this clause describes the Holy Spirit as proceeding "from the Father, *and the Son*" — they are really objecting to the pope's authority to do what they claim only an ecumenical council could do. But then if they also refuse to participate in any of the ecumenical councils convoked, either, the supreme magisterium of the Church has surely become thereby indefinitely suspended. If it were really true that the centuries of separation between the East and the West have had this real effect of suspending the Church's supreme magisterium — which nearly everybody still agrees operated authoritatively and indeed infallibly through the Councils of Nicaea, Constantinople, Ephesus, and Chalcedon — then that effective silencing of the authentic voice of Christ in the world would surely have constituted the greatest of all the calamities that could ever have stemmed from the separation.

The Catholic Church, however, could not and cannot accept the view that the Church's supreme magisterium is strictly limited to only one mode of expression that was universally accepted in the early Church (ecumenical councils). Other Christian bodies, including the Eastern Orthodox, do not really accept that view either as a practical matter. They continue to make doctrinal and moral judgments all the time; their bishops hold synods and issue judgments. The real question is, though, on what *basis* do they presume to make authoritative pronouncements on faith and morals, if the only fully accepted valid authority is that of an ecumenical council composed of representatives of the entire (undivided) Church?

The Catholic Church understands that Christ established the Church upon Peter as well as upon the other apostles, and she has also always correctly seen that she had to carry on as well as move on in order to carry out Christ's mandate to teach, govern, and sanctify, in spite of the disagreements and schisms that have unfortunately arisen among Christians themselves; or of conquests of Christian territories by non-Christian rulers; or of other obstacles and setbacks in her way.

As regards her teaching and governing authority, the Church has had to go on convening ecumenical councils, for example, regardless of whether the East was willing to participate in them or not. Similarly, the popes had to go on exercising the supreme authority conferred on Peter and his successors by Christ, regardless, again, of whether the East was prepared to accept that authority. The Church could not simply wait around until all the schisms were healed before moving on to fulfill the duties and functions confided to her by Christ. Thus, the development of the papal magisterium, as also the convening of successive ecumenical councils in the West, were developments that were strictly called for, if the Church of Christ was to meet the challenges of history and of her life in this world.

Of course we can only rejoice if, meanwhile, the Eastern Churches proved also able to preserve the Church's ancient teaching and her sacramental system. Similarly, the rich devotional and liturgical and artistic heritage of the Eastern Churches constitutes a great and noble blessing for all Christians. Vatican Council II, in particular, drew heavily upon that heritage. But these things are not enough if an exclusive adherence to accepted tradition in the East continues to render impossible in the world of today the Christian unity for which Christ prayed. Further on, when we come to discuss Pope John Paul II's 1995 encyclical *Ut Unum Sint* on Commitment to Ecumenism, we shall consider what some of the next ecumenical steps ought to be as far as the Eastern Churches are concerned. Meanwhile, we need to look at what ecumenical progress has been made with regard to the Protestant Churches and ecclesial communities with which the Catholic Church has been in dialogue since Vatican II.

CHAPTER TEN

RELATIONS WITH THE REFORMATION COMMUNIONS

THE RELATIONS OF THE Catholic Church with the Christian communions stemming from the Protestant Reformation is a subject which is more than a little paradoxical, as we have already remarked. This is the case because there has in fact been enormous "progress" in terms of dialogue, cooperation, agreed statements, services and prayers in common, and the like — all of these things along with an enormous amount of good will on all sides. None of this, however, has led, or now seems likely to lead, as far as anybody can now see, to any actual reunion. Few or no Protestant Churches or groups show any disposition to accept reunion on any terms that the Catholic Church could possibly accept. Indeed it is hard to imagine any possible reunion with them which would not have to involve some form of the old, discarded idea of a "return." For, as everybody realizes, the Protestant Churches and ecclesial communities stemming from the Reformation have *not* preserved a valid episcopal hierarchy and priesthood, nor a complete sacramental system. So it is difficult to imagine what could be the basis of any actual reunion with the Catholic Church — even while cooperation and good will continue.

Moreover, even as carefully worked out and no doubt sincere agreed statements are concluded, some Protestant communions have nevertheless gone on taking initiatives which can only make any prospects for reunion harder still, if not ultimately impossible. The Anglican Communion, for example, has allowed the ordination of women in some of its provinces since 1976; seven Anglican provinces even approve of female *bishops*. More recently, in November, 2003, the Episcopal Church USA ordained as a bishop a man who had earlier abandoned his wife and daughter to live in an open unchaste homosexual relationship with another man. A little earlier, in May, 2003, an Anglican diocese in Canada approved the public blessing of same-sex unions. These last two actions set in motion a process of what appears to be a new schism within the Anglican Communion itself — a schism for which the titular head of the Anglican Communion, the archbishop of Canterbury in England, with the best will in the world, can hardly provide a solution, lacking as he does any *"primacy of jurisdiction,"* such as the pope enjoys as head of the Catholic Church.

Meanwhile, other Protestant denominations in recent years have similarly installed openly homosexual clergy and/or blessed same-sex unions — just as some of those same denominations earlier found themselves able to sanction, if not actually bless, such other grave evils as euthanasia, legalized abortion, embryonic stem-cell research, cloning, and the like — not to speak of the already gravely evil practice of in-vitro fertilization (IVF) itself. And, of course, the general Protestant approval of contraception, sterilization, and divorce is of rather long standing. In addition to all these departures from historical Christianity, there is also the case of the formerly ecumenically serious World Council of Churches which, in recent years, has sometimes functioned more like an international leftist political pressure group than like any recognizably ecclesial body. The National Council of Churches in the United States has similarly now apparently been politicized in a leftist sense past the point, it would seem, where it can now still be taken seriously as a truly "Christian" ecumenical partner.

There is no way the Catholic Church could ever accommodate the abandonment of Sacred Scripture and the traditional moral teaching of the Church to which most of these developments point. Nevertheless, in spite of such manifest obstacles to any real prospect of reunion with those Christian bodies tracing their origin back to the Reformation, the Catholic Church still persists in pursuing with them the new ecumenism as it has been articulated and practiced since it was adopted by Vatican II in the Decree on Ecumenism, *Unitatis Redintegratio.* A whole new climate of openness and friendliness *has* replaced the hostility and even polemics that in the past so often characterized the relationships between Catholics and Protestants.

But it is, of course, also true that some continuing Protestant hostility is encountered as a result of the strong stands taken by the Catholic Church on contemporary moral issues, where many Protestants appear to have decided to follow the decadent secular culture. On the other hand, many Protestants, particularly Evangelicals, who are opposed to such contemporary evils as abortion, euthanasia, same-sex unions, cloning, and the like have come to have new respect for the Catholic Church's principles and consistency. Some of them now even look to the Church for leadership in the current culture wars. Pope John Paul II, in particular, garnered much praise and admiration for many of the visible moral stands he took in circles that once would have been thought to be highly unlikely ever to say anything positive about the Catholic Church — not to speak of the papacy! — namely, among Southern Baptists. We need think in this connection only of the Baptist leader who, speaking about John Paul II, once declared that: "The Catholic Church has a pope who knows how to pope"! There is even a very real sense in which the popes have come to be broadly recognized by non-Catholics as the *de facto* "leaders" of Christianity.

Among the Reformation-based Churches and communities, the Anglican Communion, in particular, has been very actively involved in ecumenical dialogue with the Catholic Church. In *Unitatis Redintegratio* itself, it was specifically noted that "the Anglican

Communion occupies a very special place" (UR 13). Readers of biographies of Pope John XXIII and Pope Paul VI will discover that these popes, particularly the latter, very probably really believed at one point that reunion with the Anglican Church was not only possible but perhaps was even imminent. This viewpoint proved to be a very unrealistic one, of course, as things turned out, but it was a not uncommon sentiment among not a few Catholics at the time of Vatican II. All this may now seem to be somewhat ironical in view of recent developments such as female ordination and same-sex "marriage" that we have mentioned. Nevertheless, beginning in 1966, right after the Council, the popes met more often, and issued more Common Declarations, with the archbishops of Canterbury than with any other non-Catholic Church leaders.

Archbishop of Canterbury Dr. George Carey, for example, visited the Holy See no less than six times during his dozen years in office, before he finally stepped down in June of 2002, observing during his farewell visit to John Paul II that the latter's "great courage, wisdom, and holiness of life" had, in the archbishop's words, "touched and inspired Christians throughout the world." Before that, the same Archbishop Carey had created much good will when, on January 18, 2000, he helped inaugurate the Holy Year by joining the pope at St. Paul's outside the Walls to open the Holy Door.

In addition to such summit meetings between the pope and the archbishop of Canterbury, there has been a really remarkable amount of dialogue resulting in a broad range of agreed statements issued by the Anglican-Roman Catholic International Commission of Theologians (ARCIC). This body, originally established in 1970, proved to be one of the most serious and diligent of the post-Vatican II joint theological commissions. Over the years, it has produced studies and papers on such subjects as the Eucharist, ministry and ordination, authority in the Church, and mixed marriages. After some twelve years of work, the original ARCIC wound up its work, and issued a final report summarizing the results of its extended dialogue.

A reconstituted Commission (ARCIC-II) was set up in 1982, and, beginning in the following year, issued a new series of reports that included such subjects as Christian anthropology, authority, the Church as communion, the local/universal Church, and missions. Given the really extensive study and dialogue that have gone on between Anglicans and Catholics, it is not surprising that efforts were made to try to draw together all the various threads and summarize exactly all that had been agreed to. A major effort in this regard was organized in Ontario, Canada, in May, 2000, when a group of Anglican and Catholic bishops met for a whole week of study and reflection. This particular meeting grew out of a 1996 Common Declaration of the pope and the archbishop of Canterbury, and also resulted in a document on "Communion in Mission."

Yet another Anglican-Catholic initiative came at the beginning of 2002 with the launching of yet another cooperative organization, the International Anglican-Roman Catholic Commission for Unity and Mission (IARCCUM). This new commission consisted principally of bishops and, among other things, it has been working on a common statement expressing the degree of agreement that now exists between Anglicans and Catholics as a result of all the dialogue that has taken place and all the efforts that have been exerted.

The success of both IARCCUM's work and that of the ARCIC was called into question, however, after the ordination of an active homosexual as bishop of New Hampshire by the Episcopal Church USA in November, 2003, as already mentioned above. This action brought about the cancellation by the Vatican of a major IARCCUM meeting originally scheduled to be held in February, 2004. At the same time, the current Anglican co-chairman of ARCIC happened to be none other than the main consecrator of the homosexual bishop of New Hampshire, U.S. Episcopal Church Presiding Bishop Frank Griswold, who promptly resigned as co-chairman of ARCIC, in order not to harm ecumenical relations any more than they already had been harmed by the ordination itself. While deploring the action of the Episcopal Church USA, the Catholic co-chairman of ARCIC, the archbishop of Seattle, Alexander J. Brunett, issued a statement indicating that the Catholic Church was still committed to dialogue with the Episcopalians. Nevertheless, Archbishop Brunett remarked, "If we've agreed on moral values and moral statements that are not being observed, that is a problem for our on-going dialogue, and we need to deal with that issue." This was putting it both politely and diplomatically.

Thus, it has become clear that Anglican-Roman Catholic ecumenical dialogue was far from untroubled. Yet many areas of agreement remained. As recently as May, 2005, the ARCIC issued a new agreed statement on Mary which concluded that Scripture and "ancient common traditions" contained enough evidence between them to support the Catholic dogmas of the Immaculate Conception and the Assumption and which declared that the ARCIC does "not consider the practice of asking Mary and the saints to pray for us as communion dividing." With so many areas of agreement, it might seem that there had to be fewer areas of *dis*agreement. While this might be true enough in one sense, there were still outstanding, in addition to the falling out over the female and homosexual ordination issues, other major issues such as the primacy and infallibility of the pope and the validity of Anglican orders. Thus, in spite of all the sincere effort, it was still not clear where Anglican-Catholic ecumenism was going or where it would end up.

For neither female ordination nor the acceptance of homosexual behavior (by clergy or anybody else) could ever be accepted or even tolerated by the Catholic Church. So it was not in the least surprising that, when the Episcopal Church USA announced the selection of a practicing homosexual as the next Episcopal Bishop of New Hampshire, the then chairman of the U.S. Catholic bishops' Committee for Ecumenical and Interreligious Affairs, Bishop Stephen Blaire of Stockton, California, had no choice but to issue the statement he issued on August 11, 2003, in which he made abundantly clear that:

In the light of the recent decision made at the General Convention of the Episcopal Church in the United States concerning the appointment of a bishop who professes himself to be in an active homosexual relationship, and the recognition that some local Episcopalian communities bless same-sex unions, new ecumenical challenges have been created.

These decisions reflect a departure from the common understanding of the meaning and purpose of human sexuality, and the morality of homosexual activity as found in sacred Scripture and Christian tradition.

This was surely to put it mildly. Pope John Paul II, for his part, was perhaps equally restrained in his reaction, given the magnitude of the challenge, when he received in Rome, on October 4, 2003, the new archbishop of Canterbury, Dr. Rowan Williams — here was yet another Anglican prelate paying a visit to the Holy See! On that occasion, the pope spoke quite positively of the good relations that had existed up to then between Canterbury and Rome, as well as of the undeniable ecumenical progress that had been made since Vatican II (and that we have briefly summarized here). The pontiff felt obliged to warn, however, that:

As we give thanks for the progress that has already been made, we must also recognize that new and serious difficulties have arisen on the path to unity. These difficulties are not all of a merely disciplinary nature; some extend to essential matters of faith and morals. In light of this, we must reaffirm our obligation to listen attentively and honestly to the voice of Christ as it comes to us through the Gospel and the Church's apostolic tradition. Faced with the increasing secularism of today's world, the Church must ensure that the deposit of faith is proclaimed in its integrity and preserved from erroneous and misguided interpretations.

Thus spoke Pope John Paul II in 2003. In November, 2006, Archbishop Rowan Williams of Canterbury was again in Rome for a summit meeting with Pope Benedict XVI. We shall look at the results of this later meeting towards the end of this book.

CHAPTER ELEVEN

RELATIONS WITH THE REFORMATION
COMMUNIONS (Continued)

COMING IN SECOND AFTER the ecumenical work carried on with the Anglicans, the Lutheran-Roman Catholic Commission on Unity, established as early as 1967, seems to have been the other joint theological commission that has worked most actively in the post-conciliar era, and the one that also has come up with the greatest number of agreed statements, including, beginning in 1979, a statement on the Eucharist. A statement on Justification by Faith followed in 1983. In addition to the official reports issued by this Commission, there have been other joint Catholic-Lutheran statements, notably one on papal primacy, this one going back as far as 1974, when it was issued by the World Lutheran Federation and the U.S. Bishops' Committee on Ecumenical and Interreligious Affairs.

Similarly, in 1978, representatives of the Catholic Church, the Lutheran World Federation, and the World Alliance of Reformed Churches issued a joint statement on "An Ecumenical Approach to Marriage." As with the Anglicans, the various contacts and discussions that have been carried on with the Lutherans have generally been quite positive and cordial, even though there has certainly not been any break-through agreement that might indicate that the two communions really might be on the road to reunion. Once again, though, this is not really clear, in spite of all the sincere dialogue and effort that has been invested in it.

Nevertheless, one of the most significant of all the post-conciliar ecumenical statements was surely the much discussed and commented upon Lutheran and Catholic Joint Declaration on the Doctrine of Justification that was signed in Augsburg, Germany, on October 31, 1999, by representatives of the Catholic Church and the Lutheran World Federation. Cardinal Edward I. Cassidy, then president of the Pontifical Council for Promoting Christian Unity, signed for the Catholic Church; and Bishop Christian Krause, president of the Lutheran World Federation, signed for the Lutheran side.

The timing of this statement coincided with the final preparations on both sides for the celebrations of the beginning of the Third Millennium of Christianity. The date of the signing was also supposed to be significant: October 31, Reformation Day, the anniversary of Martin Luther's nailing of his Ninety-Five Theses on the church door in Wittenberg in 1517. The place of the signing of the agreed statement was also deliberately chosen to remind the world of the 1530 Confession of Augsburg, in which the Reformation leader Philip Melanchthon tried, but did not succeed, in bridging the differences between the Catholic Church and the claims of those sixteenth-century Christian leaders who had been vigorously "protesting."

This Lutheran and Catholic Joint Declaration on Justification makes the extraordinary claim that it has been able to formulate and state the doctrine of Justification in a way that, as understood and accepted today by both the Catholic and Lutheran sides, would not have merited the condemnations, each by the other, that in fact were made by the Council of Trent and the Lutheran Confessions respectively, back in the sixteenth century.

The Joint Declaration declares that the participants in the contemporary dialogue, on both sides, do not take these mutual "condemnations lightly, nor do they disavow their own past." Catholics cannot deny the truth of the formulations of the Council of Trent.

Lutherans, presumably, feel just as obliged to hold to the formulations originally made by their confession. The question, therefore, has to be whether some of those formulations could perhaps have been made differently, with no loss of truth. The Joint Declaration makes the claim that, as a result of the ecumenical dialogue and the studies that have been conducted during the previous thirty years, it has now indeed become possible to transcend some of the differences which proved so intractable during the Reformation controversies, and which brought about the separation that has now endured for nearly half a millennium.

The way in which some of the original theological disagreements that signaled and ratified the original break can now be transcended, according the Joint Declaration, comes by the way the question is now to be formulated so that both sides can claim agreement. In place of the famous Lutheran dictum that we are saved "by faith alone" (*sola fide*), the Joint Declaration states that "together we confess: by *grace* alone, in faith in Christ's saving work, and not because of any merit on our part, we are accepted by God and receive the Holy Spirit, who renews our hearts while equipping and calling us to good works" (emphasis added).

Is this a substantive enough change to make possible an agreement that proved to be impossible in the sixteenth century? It is not possible in a brief survey such as this present chapter to give a definitive answer to this question, even if the present author were a qualified expert in the theology of Justification — which is very far from being the case! Suffice it to say that the Congregation for the Doctrine of the Faith allowed the statement to be accepted as *not contrary to received Catholic teaching*. In spite of this CDF assurance, however, many questions have been raised, and there was even a lengthy hold-up on the issuance of the statement that was insisted upon by the Congregation. This delay added up to more than a year after the basic agreement had been reached by the Catholics and Lutherans involved in the dialogue. Clarifications from both sides had to be added in an annex to the document.

One of the reasons the final agreement was deemed possible and finally acceptable, no doubt, was the "negative" way in which the whole question was stated — namely, that neither side's current understanding of the doctrine of Justification now "merits condemnation." This rather curious formulation seems to have allowed each side to declare agreement without having to state positively anything that could possibly be interpreted as diverging from any past formulations on either side in what has been a live subject of controversy for several centuries now.

However that may be, Pope John Paul II accepted the document for what it was and called it "a sound basis for continuing the ecumenical theological research for addressing the remaining problems with a better founded hope of resolving them in the future." Taking up a theme which became one of his favorite themes in the years surrounding the transition into the new millennium, the pontiff described the Lutheran-Catholic Joint Declaration on Justification as "a valuable contribution to the *purification of memory* and to our common witness" (emphasis added). This idea of a "purification of memory" — deliberately bringing something back to mind in order then to lay aside the ancient grievances surrounding it — was for John Paul II an essential step on the road to possible reunion, and as many readers will recall, this pope worked diligently in a number of areas to achieve this "purification of memory."

Also on the positive side of the dialogue with the Lutherans: what the two parties, Catholic and Lutheran, agreed to seems mostly to be a clear and admirable statement of the revealed doctrine as it has been handed down. As in the case of many other such statements, it represents a solid ecumenical achievement between Catholics and Lutherans, even if no further agreements prove possible. A key passage reads as follows:

> In faith we together hold the conviction that justification is the work of the triune God. The Father sent his Son into the world to save sinners. The foundation and

presupposition of justification is the incarnation, death, and resurrection of Christ. Justification thus means that Christ himself is our righteousness, in which we share through the Holy Spirit in accord with the will of the Father.

There can be no question but that this Lutheran-Catholic Joint Declaration on the Doctrine of Justification represents one of the high-water marks achieved since the onset of the new ecumenism following Vatican II. It is surely not the last word, however. There have been criticisms of it from both the Catholic and Lutheran sides. Some Catholics have criticized it for not going far enough in the direction of the Lutherans and others for going too far. Still, the enduring value of the Declaration can perhaps be confirmed by the fact that, in 2006, the World Methodist Council gave its assent to the Declaration, and some other Christian bodies were said to be examining it with a view to possibly giving it the same kind of assent.

All in all, then, the ecumenical activity that has followed the promulgation of *Unitatis Redintegratio* by the Second Vatican Council has surely been extraordinary by any standard. There has surely been nothing quite like it in the long history of the Church. It is not just the Catholic Church that has renewed the quest for Christian unity but other Churches and communions as well. And at least some of them may be asking themselves the question, with increasing seriousness, of just why they still *do* remain separated. Even if no instances of actual reunification have yet resulted from all the ecumenical effort that has been expended, the effort itself still has to be judged positive. Moreover, some instances of reunification still *may* result from it.

For example, some of the autonomous Eastern Churches could well decide, in their own interests and for their own good, that there is no good reason why their separation should continue to be maintained. Once a single Church decided this, others could be motivated thereby to follow suit. If, as actually seems to be the case, some

Lutherans today could conclude that the concerns of their forbears can be accommodated by new formulations of disputed doctrines, then perhaps some form of reunification might prove to be possible with at least some of them as well.

However that may be, the Catholic Church at Vatican II *committed* herself to make the effort. And so far she as been as good as her word. The evidence of the abundant ecumenical activity that has taken place in the post-conciliar era points to the conclusion that the Church intends to continue to stand firm in this commitment of hers. This was confirmed by Pope Benedict XVI who, the day after his installation, on April 25, 2005, declared to a group of representatives of other Christian communions who had attended his installation that he felt "strongly the need to reassert the irreversible commitment taken by the Second Vatican Council and pursued in recent years.... The path to the full communion desired by Jesus for his disciples entails... courage, gentleness, firmness, and hope."

CHAPTER TWELVE

POPE JOHN PAUL II'S ENCYCLICAL
UT UNUM SINT

Y ES, CHRIST PRAYED "that they all may be one... so that the world may believe that you have sent me" (Jn 17:21), and so it was no doubt inevitable that Pope John Paul II would pick up on this key passage from the Gospel of John when writing his encyclical *Ut Unum Sint* ("That they may be one") on the Church's Commitment to Ecumenism. He issued this particular encyclical on May 25, 1995, more than thirty years after Vatican II's Decree on Ecumenism, *Unitatis Redintegratio*. In the encyclical, he explained one meaning of the Gospel passage which furnished him his title by noting that "this unity, which the Lord has bestowed on his Church, and in which he wishes to embrace all peoples, is not something added on, but stands at the very heart of Christ's mission" (UUS 9).

It is worth looking carefully at this encyclical since it both describes and demonstrates what has been brought about by Vatican II's decision to adopt the new ecumenism. We should also note at the outset that the English subtitle of the encyclical is: "On the Church's Commitment to Ecumenism." *Commitment!* The Holy Father did not get very far into his subject before he reminded us that "at the Second Vatican Council the Catholic Church committed herself *ir-revocably* to following the path of the ecumenical venture" (UUS

3; italics in the original). We have already seen how diligently the Church has been following that path.

Ecumenism, the pope added a little later on, "is not just some sort of 'appendix' which is added on to the Church's traditional activity" — although this is often the way some Catholics today tend to treat it, among them Catholics who are themselves very serious and committed to the cause of the Church. The pope, however, insisted that "ecumenism is an organic part of her life and work" (UUS 20).

It would be hard to put it more strongly that, according to Pope John Paul II, ecumenism is now an integral part of the Catholic thing. It no doubt should long since have been practiced more diligently than it normally was practiced, that is, it should have been practiced in the way that it has been practiced since Vatican II. However that may be, though, it is definitely here to stay now, following the emphasis the Council placed upon it. It is in no way merely a fad or a frill.

The pope ascribed the Church's firm decision about this to the Council. Throughout the encyclical he constantly refers back to the Council. The first third of the encyclical, and more, is practically a tissue of conciliar quotations strung together. If anyone ever needed proof that Pope John Paul II was a pope of the Second Vatican Council *par excellence*, the proof could be found spelled out here in this encyclical as clearly as it could be found anywhere. It would not be inaccurate to say that the ecumenism of Pope John Paul II was virtually the same thing as the ecumenism of Vatican II.

Interestingly enough, though, as we have already noted, when we look at the Council's Decree on Ecumenism, we find in it Vatican II's strongest and clearest statement of the traditional belief that the visible Catholic Church is what we used to call "the one, true Church." Far from muting the Church's claims in the interests of harmony among Christians, the Decree made a point instead of affirming the Church's maximum claims. Just as the Council's strongest reiteration of the truth of the Catholic faith comes, perhaps ironically, in its Declaration of Religious Liberty, *Dignitatis Humanae*,[1] so the Council's strongest affirmation that the Catholic Church is, indeed, as all previous generations of Catholics have believed, "God's only flock," as the Council declares at one point (UR 2), comes nowhere else but in its Decree on Ecumenism. We cannot remind ourselves too often of the importance of this passage, precisely because it has been so often down-played and even ignored in the post-conciliar years:

> For it is through Christ's Catholic Church alone, which is the universal help towards salvation, that the fullness of the means of salvation can be obtained. It was to the apostolic college alone, of which Peter is the head, that we believe Our Lord entrusted all the blessings of the New Covenant, in order to establish on earth the Body of Christ into which all those should be incorporated who belong in any way to the people of God (UR 3).

If "all those who belong in any way to the people of God" should simply be "incorporated" into the Catholic Church, according to Vatican II, then what was it that was essentially changed from the days when the Catholic attitude towards ecumenism was more or less to wait around until everybody had seen the light and decided to *return* to the one, true fold of Christ? This, of course, is an attitude that persists among some Catholics, in spite of the Church's emphasis since Vatican II on the new ecumenism: if we have the full truth, as we do, and all the sacramental means of grace conducing to our sanctification and salvation, as we also do — and if the Church Christ established for all his disciples indeed *is* the visible Catholic Church, as is also the case — then why should we have to be both-

---

[1] "The Catholic Church is by the will of Christ the teacher of truth. It is her duty to proclaim and teach with authority the truth which is Christ and, at the same time, to declare and confirm by her authority the principles of the moral order which spring from human nature itself... in forming their consciences, the faithful must pay careful attention to the sacred and certain teaching of the Church" (DH 14).

ered with all the dialogue, the debates, the agreed statements, the prayers for unity, and such?

Similarly, why should the successor of Peter, the Vicar of Christ, have to subject himself on his visits to such things as the calculated and deliberate discourtesy, not to say the outright insults, that came to him, for example, from Greek monks or Russian prelates (some of the latter even being former KGB agents!)? Why did there have to be all of John Paul II's "apologies" for the admitted past sins of Catholics which contributed to disunity, when so few others ever seemed disposed to acknowledge *their* past sins and faults which also contributed to that separation? Weren't *they* the ones who "broke away," after all? Is it not the Catholic Church that has best preserved unity? And if we possess the fullness of the revealed truth of Christ, why should we have to endure the condescension of our sophisticated contemporaries, some of them within our own ranks, who believe that all the past, "exaggerated" claims of the Catholic Church have become passé since Vatican II anyway? These are all real and pertinent questions, but there cannot be any doubt that John Paul II had his own answers to them.

First of all, in the pope's view, we have to accept and endure all the kinds of things we suffer in the course of doing our duty because it is actually a *command* of Christ that we should continue to seek Christian unity, in spite of the obstacles that we may come up against, and in spite of the failures that we may experience. Both the pope and Council strongly assured us that this was truly our situation. There was thus no way that we could honorably avoid or evade the unpleasant and discouraging aspects — or perhaps even the "unrealistic" ones! — of attempting to pursue the new ecumenism: it has nevertheless been strictly necessary that we should keep on trying anyway. It is nothing less than the will of Christ for us. The Catholic Church, being what she is, could always in any case endure the disappointments and even rebuffs that may have come from honest ecumenical efforts. The Church cannot be diminished by seeking to do Christ's will. On the contrary: she provides thereby further proof of the truth of what she is.

More than that, too many of our fellow Christians simply do not recognize the fact that we Catholics *do* belong to the actual Church Christ founded, the Church which possesses the fullness of his truth and grace. Typically, they think *they* have it over on the Catholic Church because they adhere to the "full Gospel," or have eschewed "superstition," are not "subservient" to the pope, or don't engage in "vain repetitions" in their prayers, or haven't innovated in the area of the doctrine that has been handed down as a result of the latest findings of German scholarship, or something of the sort. They need to be *shown* that it is the Catholic Church, properly described and explained, which possesses all the lineaments of the Church Christ founded as she is described in the New Testament and in the early Fathers; they need to be convinced. It is the non-Catholics, precisely, who do not understand this; it is they who are "the lost sheep."

Thus, like the Good Shepherd in the parable, it is Catholics who have to take the risk to go out after these lost sheep. In many, if not most, cases, they are not likely to come to us. If Christ wills that his disciples be united, then it is incumbent upon those of his followers who believe they are following him most closely to attempt at least to start some kind of unity project, whether or not any immediate results can be expected. This, in fact, is what the new ecumenism which the Catholic Church has been pursuing since Vatican II is all about — the new ecumenism which Pope John Paul II expressly made one of the strongest priorities of his pontificate.

One of the principal things that the Council deliberately aimed to change was: how we Catholics are to look at those Christians outside the visible boundaries of the Catholic Church. Instead of seeing them as being simply in error, which is the almost reflexive reaction most Catholics are bound to have, the Council stressed instead that "those who believe in Christ and have been properly baptized are put in some, though imperfect, communion with the Catholic Church" (UR 3). They are related to us in a way that, for example, Muslims or Hindus or Buddhists or unbaptized unbelievers are not.

In yet other words, although baptized non-Catholic Christians do not possess the *fullness* of the truth and grace of Christ, they nevertheless possess these blessings in some measure — and this constitutes the foundation that must be built upon. The approach of both Vatican II and John Paul II to ecumenism requires that we look positively at what non-Catholics and their various communions do possess: "The separated Churches and communities, though we believe they suffer from defects, have been by no means deprived of significance and importance in the mystery of salvations" (UR 4).

Thus, according to the Council, Christians and Christian communions separated from the Catholic Church possess some, but not the "fullness," of the means of salvation. While this is an easy concept to state, it is not easy to get across in all of its implications. Contemporary religion teachers, in particular, seem to find it hard to inculcate the respect which the pope and the Council say must be given to Christian traditions outside the Catholic Church without soft-pedaling or undermining the traditional Catholic teaching that the Catholic Church is nevertheless the one, true Church of Christ. Once the uniqueness of the Church has been grasped, the temptation is to think, as many Christians have thought down through the centuries, and as St. Cyprian of Carthage plainly expressed it, that "whoever is separated from the Church is separated from the promises of the Church" (*De Catholicae Ecclesiae Unitate* 6).

In other words, if you are outside the visible Church, as is sometimes simplistically thought, you are in grave danger of not being saved — bluntly, of going to hell. The truth is, of course, that *anybody* is in grave danger of not being saved who fails to do God's will according to his lights and to what has been given to him. This applies to Catholics as much as it applies to anybody else. Moreover, we must not soft-pedal this uncomfortable truth in an era which is so prone to do so, for it is a truth and a warning that comes from the mouth of Christ himself, on numerous occasions, as reported in the Gospels. Conversely, those who do the will of Christ according the lights and the means they do possess *can* be saved, whether or not they belong to the visible Church.

What the Catholic Church established by Christ provides, however, is the best and surest *way* to salvation. The teachings of the Church provide, as it were, a *map* enabling us to locate heaven and chart our course towards it more easily — just as the sacraments of the Church provide periodic helps and guideposts on the road to that same destination. Catholics are not better than those outside the Church; as a good friend of mine has perceptively observed, they are better *off.* It is strictly speaking true that heaven can be reached without the map and the guideposts and provisions for the journey provided by the Church; but the road in that case is both harder and less sure.

Moreover, "all children of the Church should remember... that their exalted condition results not from their own merits, but from the grace of Christ. If they fail to respond in thought, word, and deed to that grace, not only shall they not be saved, but they shall be the more severely judged" (*Lumen Gentium* 14).

Thus, the *need* of sinful humanity for Christ's Church remains in all its urgency, and God in Christ has graciously and mercifully supplied that need by the gift of his Church. At the same time, as both the pope and Council teach, Christians without the fullness of Christ's truth and the means of grace which the Church supplies do possess at least *some* of the truth and of those means, although they possess them ultimately, of course, as mysteriously coming *from* the Church in a way which we cannot easily understand.

It may sometimes come about, and in many cases has come about, that individual Christians have traveled down the road to individual conversion to the Catholic Church. They have "crossed the Tiber," as the saying goes. Many do seek and come to see the light in this way. May their tribe increase! It even seems that recently it has been increasing once again, after a period which saw a relative dearth of conversions. To some extent, this new impetus to conver-

sions may have come about because of the disarray in other communions subjected to the powerful influences of our decadent modern
secular culture. It seems clear that the Catholic Church attracts serious and traditional Christians in very great part because she is perceived to have resisted today's collapse of moral standards in society
more successfully than some other Christian communions.

There still remain, however, enormous numbers of serious
Christians and Christian bodies that have *not* seen reunion with the
Catholic Church as having the same priority which John Paul II assigned to it, nor with the same urgency with which Christ prayed for
it. By accepting them as authentic Christians and worthy dialogue
partners, in accordance with the Council and the post-conciliar
popes, we have not merely changed *our* approach; *their* view of us
has in many respects been significantly changed as well. An increasing number of non-Catholic Christians now seem disposed to view
us as authentic Christians as well. Many Catholics have had actual
experiences of this new attitude towards Catholicism and the Catholic Church, for example, in the contemporary pro-life movement.

We do not, of course, know what the final outcome of this new
era of good feeling among Christians will be — whether or not it will
actually lead to Christian unity. But to the extent that Evangelicals,
for example, are now prepared to see Catholics as fellow Christians,
it has to be said that progress has been made. Similarly, Pope John
Paul II's dramatic "apologies" for past Catholic sins delivered in
places such as Greece and Israel had notable effects on how Catholics and the Church are viewed in those places today. Pope John Paul
II, in particular, had an uncanny ability to *disarm* his critics, and the
critics of the Church. In his case, many who came to scoff *did* stay
around to pray. Besides, why is it not anything but to the great credit
of the Catholic Church also to be the Christian body that has volun-
tarily and very publicly tried to *remove* some of the obvious existing
obstacles in the way of possible Christian reunion?

All of these things, of course, have significantly changed the
ecumenical climate in recent years. Even though we may have no

significant examples of actual reunion to hold up after nearly forty years of the new ecumenism, we must still be thankful to Vatican II and to the post-conciliar popes for having led the Church into a new era in which there are now at least some tangible hopes of some day seeing realized Christ's prayer for the unity of all Christians. The Council and the post-conciliar popes have at the very least obliged us to begin to take this prayer of Christ's a little more *seriously*! We need to continue on in that vein.

CHAPTER THIRTEEN

POPE JOHN PAUL II'S ENCYCLICAL
UT UNUM SINT (Continued)

S OME THIRTY YEARS AFTER the end of the Council, then, on
March 25, 1995, Pope John Paul II produced his remarkable
encyclical, *Ut Unum Sint* ("That They May Be One"), clearly
intending thereby to give further impetus to the Church's ecumenical efforts as the Third Millennium of Christianity approached. The
Polish pope firmly believed, and said, that "despite our divisions,
we are on our way towards full unity, that unity which marked the
Apostolic Church at its birth..." (UUS 23). Even though we might
look around and wonder if the Holy Father was perhaps not exagger-
ating just a little bit here, we must nevertheless concede that his very
assurance and conviction effectively served to drive the ecumenical process forward, both for Catholics and for at least some of the
other Christians with whom the Church has been engaged in serious
dialogue. Faced with our contemporary "culture of death," for example, the moral leadership alone provided by the bishop of Rome,
in the sight of the whole world, had a profound effect on Christians
everywhere. By himself and by his sheer determination, John Paul
II succeeded in changing many of the terms of contemporary ecumenical relations.

We noted earlier that Vatican II had laid out four ecumenical
tasks for Christians:

- "To avoid expressions, judgments, and actions which do not represent the condition of our separated brethren with truth and fairness."

- To conduct "dialogue between competent experts from different churches" in order to gain "truer knowledge and more just appreciation."

- To engage in more intensive cooperation for the common good, including common prayer.

- "To examine [our] faithfulness to Christ's will for the Church and, wherever necessary, undertake with vigor the task of renewal and reform" (UR 4).

Of these four tasks enjoined by the Council, Pope John Paul II, in *Ut Unum Sint,* emphasized the one he considered more important than any of the others, namely, *prayer.* Yes: he considered prayer to be the *basis* for ecumenical dialogue (UUS 21-27). Nor was he ever anything but utterly serious about this. He always considered the joint prayer services in which he participated, whether with Southern Baptists or Eastern Orthodox — and everyone in between — to be of the greatest importance for the Church's on-going ecumenical effort. In November, 2003, for example, on the occasion of a plenary assembly of the Pontifical Council for Promoting Christian Unity, he reminded those present:

> Forty years after the celebration of the Second Vatican Council, when many of the pioneers of ecumenism have already entered the Father's House, we can see in looking back over the ground covered that we have come a long way and have entered the very heart of the divisions, exactly where they hurt most. This has come about, above all, thanks to prayer (*L'Osservatore Romano* - English Edition, December 3, 2003).

Meanwhile, however, John Paul II did not neglect the question of doctrinal truth. His statements on this subject in *Ut Unum Sint* ought to satisfy even those who are most skeptical about the ecumenical prospects, those who wonder (and sometimes with reason in the case of some of those perhaps too enthusiastically and uncritically given over to the "dialogue") whether all the post-Vatican II emphasis on ecumenism might not lead to the watering down of the deposit of faith. Whatever the risk of this — though it hasn't shown up in any of the Church's *official* documents — the pope, for his part, remained firm and clear in his commitment both to the new ecumenism *and* to the integrity of Catholic truth. He wrote in this regard, very plainly:

> The unity willed by God can be attained only by the adherence of all to the content of the revealed faith in its entirety. In matters of faith, compromise is in contradiction with God, who is truth (UUS 18).

Or again, farther along in the text of the encyclical, he wrote:

> Full communion... will have to come about through the acceptance of the whole truth into which the Holy Spirit guides Christ's disciples. Hence all forms of reductionism or facile "agreement" must be absolutely avoided (UUS 36).

However tempted others of those engaged in the dialogue might be to water down difficult truths in order to reach agreement, it cannot be said that John Paul II — who was responsible for overseeing the whole ecumenical process on the Catholic side, after all — was ever tempted in the slightest to mute or downplay any received Catholic doctrine, even as he remained an absolutely convinced proponent of continuing to engage in ecumenical dialogue. His continuing strong personal emphasis on *Marian devotions* similarly testified to his retention of traditional Catholic religious practice even as he sought greater ecumenical understanding and agreement.

Much of the second part of the encyclical *Ut Unum Sint* is devoted to the Holy Father's own account of the ecumenical prog-

ress which he believed had already taken place up to the time of
the writing of the encyclical, particularly with regard to the Eastern Orthodox Churches. As he saw it, these Churches continued in
possession of the apostolic succession, true sacraments, and a valid
priesthood, and therefore, in his view, there *had* to be a way to become reconciled with them. This was his attitude. In the encyclical, he discussed at length the modern ecumenical relations with
the Orthodox that began in 1965 with the mutual lifting of the joint
excommunications of pope and patriarch that had dated back to the
year 1054.

John Paul II believed that further ecumenical progress had
been made following this 1965 reconciliation. His strong belief in
this regard no doubt underlay his willingness, indeed, his insistence,
in pressing on with his ecumenical agenda — and also in continuing
his journeys to Orthodox lands, even in the face of the rebuffs he
more than once encountered. Even on these trips, though, he often
retained his ability to disarm his critics and critics of the Catholic
Church. (Though he was not, in the end destined to get to Moscow,
as we have noted, perhaps a successor of his just might finally make
it there.)

In addition to the major effort John Paul II made to be reconciled with the Eastern Orthodox Churches, he was particularly proud
of the contacts and agreements made by himself and his predecessors, Pope John XXIII and Pope Paul VI, with the Ancient Eastern
Churches, among them the Copts of Egypt, Ethiopia, and Eritrea,
the Syrian Orthodox Church, the Armenian Orthodox Church, and
the Assyrian Church of the East. We have already covered some of
this same territory that the pope covered in his encyclical regarding the renewed relations with these ancient communions separated
from Constantinople as well as from Rome. It is no longer clear, for
example, what differences of *faith* even remain between the Catholic
Church and what some of these Ancient Eastern Churches have now
agreed to. The dialogues that have been conducted with them suggest
that we substantially *do* agree with them on the faith concerning the

Christological questions that led to their separation in ancient times. The time may indeed be ripe for reunion. It could actually be that one or more of them will accept full communion with the Catholic Church, papal primacy and all — and sooner than we might think. They have little or no *vested interest* in continued separation! We should also not forget that the "Orthodox Church" really consists of some fourteen or so autonomous and autocephalous Churches, each one of which *could* also at some point decide that reunion with the bishop of Rome, as in ancient times, would be worth the problems that would arise for any "autonomous" Orthodox Church that might ever decide to try it. Pope John Paul II certainly thought about such things as he pursued his ecumenical efforts. His hopes with regard to reunion with the "Orthodox" were far from simple illusions. After all, even the Orthodox leaders mostly continued to receive him — as they themselves continued to be cordially received at the Vatican on an increasingly regular basis.

In looking at the progress that has been made in the East, however, it is worth pointing out another fact that the pope fully recognized and accepted, just as Vatican II also did (cf. UR 16). The fact in question is this: any Eastern Church that might ever enter into communion with the Catholic Church, would have the right to self-governance; and, even under the Roman primacy, would have its own "organizational structures" (UUS 60) — much as, for example, the Maronite Catholics already do have under their patriarch in Lebanon. The pope would simply not be involved in the direct governance of these Churches — certainly not as directly as he has been in the Western Church.

Rather, as John Paul II explicitly said, quoting Vatican II, "if disagreements in belief and discipline arose" among the Churches accepting communion with the Catholic Church, the Roman See would act "by common consent as *moderator*" (UR 14; UUS 95; emphasis added). As John Paul II pointed out, "for a whole millennium Christians were united in [this] 'brotherly communion of faith and sacramental life'" (*Ibid.*).

The special importance which John Paul II placed on reunion with the Eastern Orthodox can be seen in the space allotted to them in his encyclical. He devoted four substantial sections to them (UUS 50-61), while allotting only one section each to the Ancient Churches of the East (UUS 62-63) and to the Churches and ecclesial communities in the West (UUS 64-70). Nevertheless, in *Ut Unum Sint,* the pope also expressed his hopes for serious reunion with the Churches and ecclesial communities of the West, nearly all of which stem from the Protestant Reformation of the sixteenth century. This, of course, is a subject much closer to those of us who live in the United States. John Paul II believed that the near universal Christian recognition and acceptance of the sacrament of baptism provided the basis for further dialogue — as did the celebration of the Lord's Supper in at least some of the Protestant denominations (UUS 66).

It is true that these features of Protestant worship scarcely provide common ground as wide as that provided by the worship of the Eastern Churches. Nevertheless, the pope recognized also the great importance of continuing Protestant respect and reverence for the revealed Word of God in the Scriptures. He noted in the encyclical that "these brothers and sisters promote love and veneration for the Sacred Scriptures," (UUS 66); and he quoted *Unitatis Redintegratio* to the effect that Protestants, correctly and laudably, "affirm the divine authority of the sacred books" (UR 21).

It could be, of course, in God's Providence, that unity with members of the Churches and ecclesial communities stemming from the Reformation, lacking as they do, a valid priesthood and sacraments, could nevertheless come about through the "old" tried and true method of individual conversions. Here we need to mention the Protestant minister in Michigan who recently not only converted, but brought most of his congregation along with him into the Catholic Church! He had begun a project with his congregation looking at the features of "the early Church," and before they were through, they discovered that "the early Church" *was* the Catholic Church!

For the better relations among separated Christians that have been encouraged since Vatican II cannot but enhance the prospects for individual conversions. Serious believers in Christ, some of whose denominations are currently busy casting off various essential features of historic Christianity, surely need some place to go. We must pray and strive that *we* will never be the obstacle in the way of their seeing the Catholic Church as the place to go.

There is one more final short point to be made before we move to the next chapter to look at the Roman primacy in ecumenical perspective, as Pope John Paul II treated this question in his *Ut Unum Sint*. But the pope also remarked in the encyclical, significantly, that in the bloody century of totalitarianisms and their victims that the twentieth century turned out to be, all Christians "already have a common martyrology" (UUS 84). The pope returned to this same theme in one of the sermons he delivered in Armenia during his visit there in September, 2001: "You understand that where Christians were suffering," the pope said, "though divided among themselves, there already existed a profound unity." The modern totalitarian persecutors of Christians have generally *not* distinguished between Catholics, Protestants, or Orthodox — or members of one of the Ancient Churches of the East. *That*, surely, ought to constitute at least some kind of a new basis for Christian unity. So John Paul II profoundly believed. Christians of all persuasions sharing a "common martyrology" certainly also thereby shared, in his view, improved prospects for actual reunion!

CHAPTER FOURTEEN

THE ENCYCLICAL AND THE ROMAN PRIMACY

THE MOST DIFFICULT ecumenical question discussed in Pope John Paul II's encyclical *Ut Unum Sint*, as in the life of the Churches themselves, still remained (and remains) to be dealt with: this is the question of the primacy of the Roman pontiff over the universal Church. This is the often overriding question that has kept separation alive for centuries. While many non-Catholics continue to reject out of hand the very idea of it, everyone on all sides also really knows that the Catholic Church continues to insist on it before all else. Practically the only thing that many otherwise well-informed Catholics even know about *Ut Unum Sint* (and some of them do not approve) is that, in the encyclical, the pope raised the question of how "to find a new way of exercising the primacy" (UUS 95).

Sincere Catholics have almost inevitably had to ask: What was wrong with the old way? The Holy See, and the long succession of supreme pontiffs who have occupied Peter's chair down through the centuries, have quite amazingly — and, some serious students of Church history would even be tempted to add, "sometimes almost miraculously" — succeeded in preserving and handing down intact, through the events and vicissitudes of some twenty centuries, the authentic faith and sacraments confided by Jesus Christ himself to his Church. Objectively, it *is* an absolutely amazing story, by any historical standard.

Yet in spite of the unique historical record of the papacy in preserving and handing on the authentic faith which Christ confided to the care of the apostles, many Christians are not only not sold on the papacy; they consider it a prime example of the corruption of the faith, as they understand it. It is well known that, beginning with the Reformation, Protestants have consistently tended to reject the very idea of the papacy. "Popery" summed up everything that was to be objected to in the religious history of the British Isles, for example.

Catholics, however, for their part, are just as likely to see the faith of many such Protestant Christians, however sincere and even fervent it might be on its own terms, as truncated and impoverished, lacking, as it so often does, the fullness of all the sacraments, especially the holy Eucharist, as well as the fullness of Christ's authentic teaching. And meanwhile, Catholics cannot help but notice how the original faith *has* tended to get watered down, and the body of Christ to get splintered, where the principles of the Reformation have held sway. These considerations, however, seem not to have mattered much to Protestants, if they ever registered much with them at all.

And all this time Eastern Christians have tended to see the papacy as an abuse or usurpation of power, even as a "tyranny." Even though they may have retained the sacraments and the priesthood and the episcopacy, Eastern Christians tend to see the way Rome has historically handled and developed the authority possessed by its bishops as illegitimate and unwarranted. If there is one thing that non-Catholic Christians generally agree with each other about, in spite of *their* mutual disagreements, it is that the greatest single obstacle to any thought of possible reunion with the Catholic Church lies in the position and primacy of the pope.

It is surely significant that, throughout all the dialogue and agreed ecumenical statements and such that have been concluded since the new ecumenism was inaugurated at Vatican II some forty plus years ago, scarcely a single one ever attempts to deal directly with the question of the primacy. In many ways, it remains the now proverbial huge elephant in the living room that people keep trying not to notice.

Pope John Paul II, however, like Paul VI before him, was not loath to raise the question. In the encyclical *Ut Unum Sint*, the pope offered to engage in what he called "a patient and fraternal dialogue" with "pastors and theologians" of other Churches (UUS 96) in order to find a way of satisfying their well-known and often expressed objections to the position occupied by the pope. Nor should we imagine that the Polish pope was anything but serious about the dialogue he proposed to the leaders of these other Churches about his own role and position in the Catholic Church, and about the way in which he should be exercising his unique authority. He repeated, and quite emphatically, the same offer during his visit to Armenia in September, 2001, in these words:

> Conscious of the relevance of the ministry of the bishop of Rome in search for Christian unity, I have asked — in my encyclical letter *Ut Unum Sint* — that the bishops and theologians of our Churches reflect on the "forms in which this ministry may accomplish a service of love recognized by all concerned" (Address during the Ecumenical Liturgy in Yerevan, Armenia, September 26, 2001, quoting UUS 95).

The reaction of many Catholics to the first media reports of what Pope John Paul II seemed to be proposing in *Ut Unum Sint* — it was certainly the first reaction of the present writer — was: How can he do this? Everybody knows that the primacy of the pope over the whole Church has been infallibly *defined*, and thus surely settled for all time, by the First Vatican Council in 1870. How could a pope ever possibly go back on this? How could he even think of trying to get around such a solemn definition?

Moreover, the pope's proposal did not seem to be really addressed to anyone who could effectively respond to it. Few of the leaders or theologians of other Christian Churches and communions seemed terribly interested in it or prepared to take the pope up on his proposal in the special way it was proposed, that is, to be considered above and beyond the regular dialogue the various international theological commissions had been engaged in. Although a few non-Catholic theologians and Church leaders made some mention of the pope's offer, very probably some or even most of them did not seem to know what to make of it, and some of them were perhaps even embarrassed by the pope's suddenly, disconcertingly, moving beyond today's by-now fairly comfortably established ecumenical conventions. What could they possibly say? This pope was always coming up with unusual and sometimes very surprising initiatives!

Nor, among the non-Catholic Christian leaders who did publicly respond to the pope's initiative, did there seem to be any great enthusiasm expressed. Where public responses were forthcoming, they tended to be reiterations of long-established positions. Ecumenical Patriarch Bartholomew I of Constantinople, for example, speaking in Switzerland in December, 1995, repeated the standard traditional Eastern Orthodox position that all bishops are equally successors of the apostles and that no bishop could therefore be "over" any other bishop. Although this was no doubt the inevitable response from the East, and should perhaps have been expected, it was nevertheless disappointing, at least in part because some Eastern Orthodox theologians have by now recognized that some form of primacy in the Church is not only possible; it has admittedly actually been practiced by Eastern Orthodox patriarchs and metropolitans, who themselves have exercised various kinds and degrees of authority "over" other bishops. Historically, this has been especially true of the predecessors of Bartholomew himself in the see of Constantinople.

Of course, nothing equivalent to the supreme "primacy of jurisdiction" which Catholic teaching claims for the bishop of Rome has been admitted in the East, either in theory or in practice. Indeed, it is the "primacy of jurisdiction" claimed by the bishop of

Rome, as defined by the First Vatican Council, which other Christian Churches and communions specifically reject, and usually almost reflexively — and also with virtual unanimity. Reacting to the pope's encyclical, Konrad Raiser, general secretary of the World Council of Churches, declared that the objection was not to the way the primacy has been exercised by the popes but to the very fact that the teaching of the Church claims that the pope possesses such a primacy and that his *ex cathedra* teachings are infallible.

Some of the other reactions to the pope's initiative simply confirmed the fact that many of the Church's potential dialogue partners among Christian leaders see the very existence of any primacy as the *problem*. The secretary general of the Reformed World Alliance flatly declared that it was simply impossible to accept the papacy as the symbol of Christian unity, while the Anglican Center in Rome echoed this same judgment, namely, that the Catholic Church will not be accepted by other Christian bodies as long as she continues her claim to be the one, true Church of Christ.

The prospects of overcoming these kinds of objections any time soon thus did not seem auspicious at the time the encyclical *Ut Unum Sint* was issued in 1995; nor does the situation seem to have improved in any way since then as far as this issue of the primacy is concerned. As things stand, the changes the pope would have to make in order to make the primacy acceptable continue to be, evidently, changes that the pope *cannot* make. Some progressive Catholic theologians have even concluded from this that the objections to the primacy from outside the Church represent the real, unchangeable factors in the situation — not the dogmatically defined Church positions; and that it is the Catholic Church, therefore, that will *have* to change as the price of the desired unity.

Meanwhile, one of the other notable public reactions to the pope's proposal, in fact, seems to have come from a retired American Catholic archbishop, John R. Quinn, formerly the head of the San Francisco archdiocese. He was critical of what he evidently considered to be undue Vatican interference or micro-management of certain of the affairs of the Catholic Church in the United States. He responded to the pope's proposal in a rather ostentatious Oxford University lecture, followed by a pretentious book advocating greater "decentralization" of papal authority. *That* was evidently the way the pope was supposed to be exercising his primacy differently, according to Archbishop Quinn!

It was not long after the appearance of Archbishop Quinn's book, however, that the first revelations of widespread and uncorrected clerical sex abuse in the Church in the United States began to be revealed in the exposés of the *Boston Globe*, among other media outlets. These exposés, it will be recalled, began in earnest in January 2002. It soon became obvious that the typical "management" of the Church's affairs by the American bishops hardly lent any credence at all to the idea that *they* ought to be *more* independent of the Holy See! Archbishop Quinn himself, a one-time president of and long-time leader in the American bishops' conference, surely even bore some measure of responsibility for helping develop the "culture" of the American bishops' conference, which proved to be so apparently clueless and deficient in dealing with the scandal of clerical sex abuse — as was also the case in its defective management of other persistent problems such as, e.g., widespread theological dissent from, and clerical, religious, and academic disobedience towards, Church authority. And this was not even to speak of the prominent "Catholic" politicians and public figures to be regularly found in the ranks of those advocating and supporting such aberrations as legalized abortion and so-called "same-sex marriage".

More freedom from Roman oversight was hardly, on the record, what the American bishops needed. On the contrary, the wisdom of Christ in setting up the Church in the way that he did, with the successors of the apostles being clearly subject to the oversight and scrutiny of the successor of Peter, became resoundingly evident in the clerical sex abuse crisis, as it had not, perhaps, been quite as evident before for not a few years. In a not unimportant sense, Rome regularly helped *save* the American bishops from some of the consequences of their mistakes. Nevertheless, the same tired old theme of too much Roman "centralization" was still being echoed at the Synod of Bishops as late as October, 2001, where a number of bishops, chiefly from North America or Europe — bishops from the less developed world tend to be appreciative of Roman interventions and support — again complained about Roman centralization and called for greater "subsidiarity" in the Church. Subsidiarity, of course, is fine, and is indeed called for, provided the pastors of the Church at all levels are functioning properly. But Roman oversight has nevertheless proved to be *essential* in the post-conciliar era.

The negative or lukewarm responses by Catholic leaders to the pope's initiative calling for a re-examination of how the papal primacy should be exercised, of course, missed the whole point and purpose of what the pope was trying to do with *Ut Unum Sint*. The pope was trying to get the leaders of other Christian Churches and communions to look at and address with new seriousness the question of why they were not in communion with the Catholic Church headed by the successor of Peter, the bishop of Rome. Christ *did,* after all, set up the Church on the apostles with Peter at their head. How can this fundamental fact continue to be ignored? What real reasons are there for *not* hearing and heeding Christ's solemn prayer for Christian unity? Surely these are legitimate questions that call for serious ecumenical debate. Custom or inertia or alleged Roman errors or excesses or "power grabs" in the past surely *cannot* be considered valid reasons for the continued separation of Christians in our current "post-Christian" era.

And in any case — with regard to the move by some North American and European Catholic bishops to complain about over-centralization or Vatican micro-management — when Catholic bishops or a national Catholic bishops' conference fail to carry out their own responsibilities, then it is precisely the pope's *job* to step in with corrective measures. This is one of the important things the primacy of the successor of Peter *supposes*! It constitutes a powerful argument *in favor of* the primacy of Rome in the universal Church.

Our separated brethren ought to be able to see and appreciate this as an enormous *benefit*. The Anglican Communion, for example, could surely have profited, and could profit still, from this kind of intervention, once one of its provinces had decided to ordain a homosexually active bishop and yet another one of its provinces had decided to "bless" immoral same-sex unions! This disarray in the Anglican Communion continues on today and threatens further and continuing large-scale splits and splinters, if not actual schisms. And all of these things would seem to admit of no reasonable solutions at all, since there is precisely lacking any means or mechanism in their communion to deal with this kind of problem. The same thing can surely be said of the typical Protestant tendency simply to divide into additional denominations and sects when disagreements arise that cannot be resolved. Christ's prayer that they all may be one is simply made a mockery of in such cases.

The Orthodox Churches also are only too likely to face the same kinds of problem as soon as one (or more) of their number ever descends into any such aberration as approving, say, openly homosexual bishops or female ordination. Although such things have apparently posed few problems for the Orthodox Churches up to now, there is no guarantee that this situation will continue, given the new freedom of many of these formerly once largely government-controlled Churches today. The equality of all the bishops with each other, with no authority anywhere *over* them, is not going to help if and when such disagreements arise. Even though no such aberrations as we have mentioned are currently a problem as far as the Orthodox are concerned, these or still other aberrations as yet unforeseen could arise in these venerable communions, now that the relentless liberal drive for "modernity" is running so roughshod nearly everywhere. How are the newly liberated Orthodox Churches going to deal with what will surely be rising demands among their own faithful for the supposed new benefits of, say, modern contraceptives or recourse to today's various modern fertility-enhancing procedures?

Catholics in the United States, for example, can only rejoice at some of the actions which the Holy See has taken over the past generation with regard to the Catholic Church in the United States. It is not clear *where* we would be today — for instance, with respect to radical feminism — if the Holy See had not intervened in what the American Catholic bishops apparently thought they had to do to appease "women." The same thing can be said for abuses in the liturgy, as well as the Holy See's various interventions to try to turn back Catholic universities in America towards authentic Catholicity. The same thing can be said with regard to a number of other areas in the Church's life as well; for example, deficient catechesis, or religious instruction, which for so many years seemed incapable of solution as long as the American liberal "catechetical establishment" remained in place — until, again, the Holy See finally commissioned and published the *Catechism of the Catholic Church*, which now provides the standard of what religious instruction needs to cover. Where *would* the Catholic Church in the United States be if it were not for the wise and prudent actions of the Holy See over the past turbulent decades?

Not incidentally, at least some of our fellow Christians, viewing the negative side of all this and the rapid disintegration of traditional Christianity in their denominations, have sometimes reached the point of envying us *because* we have a pope, *habemus papam!* The popes of our day — not only John Paul II — have provided not a few proofs of why Christ strictly *needed* to assign to Peter and his successors the task of safeguarding the faith and practices of the faithful.

Nevertheless, in spite of the obvious need for the pope as, demonstrably, the most successful historical guarantor of Christian doctrinal integrity, Pope John Paul II's proposal in *Ut Unum Sint* for ecumenical dialogue specifically directed towards the manner of how the papal primacy should be exercised simply did *not* result in any major talks or breakthroughs in his pontificate, even though there were eventually a few signs that some other Church leaders

were finally beginning to consider his idea and even take it seriously. This was the case particularly among the Eastern Churches
and also among some Lutherans. There have been voices in these
communions attesting both to the need for a center of Christian
unity and recognizing that Rome perhaps *is* the obvious center of
such unity. It is just that, up to now, the conditions that Rome would
necessarily have to require in the case of such recognition have not
been accepted.

Further on we shall have to look more deeply into this whole
central question of the primacy of the pope and how it continues
to affect the prospects for Christian reunion. It is an issue that will
not go away. In the meantime, however, we should definitely *not*
conclude that the pope's proposal was ill-considered or is destined
to ultimate failure. The process is still ongoing. It may even turn
out to be that, once again, Pope John Paul II may have succeeded
in *disarming his critics* with this unprecedented proposal in his encyclical!

For in an important sense, the burden has been shifted from
what the Catholic Church was supposedly attempting to "impose"
on everybody else in order to achieve unity, namely, papal primacy,
to what other Christians might now think could or ought to be done
in order to achieve the unity for which everybody now seems to
agree that Christ did pray. "If you object so strongly to the Roman
primacy as exercised by the popes," the pope was saying, in effect,
to serious non-Catholic Christians, "then tell us how *you* think the
unity for which Christ prayed so fervently *is* supposed to be brought
about and maintained"!

The whole business about the pope's famous "apologies" for
past Catholic "sins" is pertinent here as well, for the pope admitted,
in effect, that the Roman primacy had *not* always been as well or
effectively exercised down through history as it should have been.
Thus, the logical question that should arise in the minds of all Christians desirous of Christian unity has to be: how *should* it be exercised then? At the same time, we should perhaps not forget that

merely to ask the question seriously is already to *grant the existence of the primacy*!

In this connection, the fact that some progress has been made since Vatican II with regard to the primacy can be seen by reference to the incident when, commenting on the discussion of the matter during the Third Session of the Council, the prominent Protestant Professor Oscar Cullmann declared that he saw virtually no chance for the recognition of the papal primacy by Protestants — though he believed at the same time that ecumenical dialogue should nevertheless proceed anyway in order to determine what points of ecumenical agreement could be reached. A noted exegete who had taught at both the Universities of Paris and of Basel, Cullmann believed that ecumenical dialogue would at least bring out what the differences really were; only then could any such thing as possibly settling any of these differences be considered. He declared:

> I have always said that the real union of the Churches is impossible at the present time because their very conception of unity is different, and is rooted in our faiths as Protestants and Catholics respectively. To ask the pope to accept our conception and give up the primacy would be tantamount to asking him to become a Protestant. Likewise, to ask Protestants to submit to the Roman conception of primacy would be to ask them to cease being Protestants. Our real ecumenical task, on the contrary, is to come closer together and continue the dialogue on unity and primacy, without obliging the pope to abandon his claim to primacy, which is guaranteed by the Roman conception of apostolic succession, and without obliging Protestants to recognize it.

In other words, Professor Cullmann, like the Fathers of Vatican II when they adopted the new ecumenism, was prepared to endorse an open-ended ecumenical dialogue, even while being somewhat skeptical of, or at least leaving open, the prospect of whether any possible permanent results might ever stem from it. Whatever else might be said of such a stance, it surely cannot be said that it is incompatible with *faith*!

Moreover, nearly forty years of ecumenical dialogue demonstrably *have* brought Catholics and Protestants closer together, even if ultimate unity still eludes them. On the question of the primacy itself, where it is hard to see how most Protestants, with their conception of an "invisible" Church, could ever accede to the very visible type of primacy that the pope does exercise over the Churches subject to him, we presumably have to go on with the open-ended dialogue that has been the norm up to now; we will certainly never be any *worse* off as a consequence. This dialogue has clearly brought out, for example, that the Anglicans, Lutherans, and Eastern Orthodox each have a somewhat *different* view of the primacy as well as of the possibility of its acceptance by non-Catholic Churches and communions. Where the dialogue might still lead *is* "open-ended."

Meanwhile, it needs to be stressed that John Paul II's own discussion of what he called in his encyclical "the Ministry of Unity of the Bishop of Rome" (UUS 86-98) gives nothing whatsoever away of the Church's defined doctrine of the primacy of jurisdiction of the See of Peter over the whole Church of Christ. The pope did not give any of this away for the simple reason that he *could not* give any of it away. He plainly stated in the encyclical that the doctrine is *unchangeable*, that the primacy is here to stay no matter what (UUS 97). His proposal to other Church leaders deals only with the practical question of how to exercise the primacy which he takes for granted is irrevocably established in the Church. Ultimately, other Christian bodies will have to accept it in whatever way proves acceptable both to them and to the authority of the Catholic Church, if they truly desire Christian unity — because the question of the primacy is indeed *not* going to go away.

In fact, the discussion of the primacy in the encyclical itself constitutes on of the most eloquent, short descriptions ever of the Church's *need* for an effective center of unity, as well as of the *fact* that Jesus Christ did, in fact, establish such a center of unity in the mission that he confided to the head apostle, Peter, and thus to his successors, the popes, in the See of Rome. The whole discussion of the primacy by John Paul II is something that needs to be read in its original form in the encyclical (UUS 86-98); only a brief sample of it can be quoted here:

> Among all the Churches and Ecclesial Communities, the Catholic Church is conscious that she has preserved the ministry of the Successor of the Apostle Peter, the Bishop of Rome, whom God established as her "perpetual and visible principle and foundation of unity" (*Lumen Gentium* 23) and whom the Spirit sustains in order that he may enable all the others to share in this essential good. In the beautiful expression of Pope Saint Gregory the Great, "my ministry is that of a *servus servorum Dei*" ["servant of the servants of God"]. This designation is the best possible safeguard against the risk of separating power (and, in particular, the primacy) from ministry. Such a separation would contradict the very meaning of power according to the Gospel: "I am among you as one who serves" (Lk 22:27; UUS 88).

Thus, the pope presented the primacy not as a form of power — let us say, power accumulated, perhaps illegitimately, by the medieval popes, as some still believe — but rather as a charge given by Christ to Peter, as the New Testament attests, and as has been faithfully maintained in the Church ever since. In the encyclical, John Paul II reviewed all of the scriptural evidence to the effect that the Church of Rome is indeed the Church of Peter and Paul, and he did not fail to cite the classical scriptural passages about Peter as the Rock on whom the Church is built and who possesses the keys of the kingdom of heaven (Mt 16:13-19); as the apostle whom Satan insisted on "having," but for whom Jesus prayed, and who is to confirm his brethren when he has "turned again" (Lk 22:31-32);

and as the apostle from whom Christ elicited the threefold profession of love and to whom he gave the command to feed the sheep
(Jn 21:15-17).

There is not the slightest suggestion in John Paul II's treatment
of the subject, then, that the primacy could ever be anything else but
what it manifestly is. The point and purpose of the discussion is how
to get non-Catholic Christians — whose seriousness and sincerity
is taken for granted for the purposes of the discussion — to *see,* and
to *accept*, what the primacy is. The pope did not make it up; nor did
he propose to give up or get around anything; he proposed only to
give over any past Catholic habit, custom, prejudice, or even blindness that may have historically contributed to the rejection of the
primacy by some Christians — and may still be preventing some of
them from accepting the primacy as something coming from Christ
in his commissioning of Peter.

There is, of course, also, a fair amount of past *non*-Catholic
habit, custom, prejudice, and even blindness that presumably would
have to be overcome as well. That is what the pope was trying to
do; he was trying to get our separated brethren to consider whether
the primacy does not, in fact, make eminently good sense. As he
explicitly stated in the encyclical, he believed that more and more of
them *were* coming to accept his conclusion (UUS 89). If, ultimately,
he failed in the course of his own pontificate to achieve the unity
for which he prayed and strived so mightily, at least he left a legacy
which cannot but contribute to Christian unity eventually — if, in
fact, it is God's will that Christian unity should come about in the
way envisaged by the Fathers of Vatican II *and* by the many non-
Catholic Christians engaged with the Catholic Church in ecumenical dialogue in the post-conciliar era. All in all, though, it has to
be said that the ecumenical performance of John Paul II — from
whom we became accustomed to witnessing not a few regular virtuoso performances! — was, here again, certainly nothing less than
that: a virtuoso performance.

One point of the pope's proposal that Christians of good will should reconsider the question of the primacy of Rome is that no Christian desirous of the unity for which Christ prayed can really say where *else* the primacy, or the Church's center of unity, might possibly be located. Serious Christians *have* to consider what, historically, the Roman primacy has been, and is, and how it has functioned. Over time John Paul II's remarkable proposal in *Ut Unum Sint* that separated Christian leaders should consider whether a kind of exercise of the primacy that all could agree upon might not, indeed, be possible may well come to be seen in the future as *the* crucial milestone in the quest for Christian unity.

Vatican II's Decree on Ecumenism, *Unitatis Redintegratio,* then, launched the new ecumenism as an irrevocable commitment of the Catholic Church. Pope John Paul II's 1995 encyclical *Ut Unum Sint* on Commitment to Ecumenism showed how far ecumenism was able to travel in the first thirty-plus years or so after the end of Vatican II. We have by no means seen the end of all this yet. In fact, we may have been witnessing only the beginning.

CHAPTER FIFTEEN

AN EASTERN ORTHODOX THEOLOGIAN RESPONDS TO THE POPE'S ENCYCLICAL

WHEN POPE JOHN PAUL II in *Ut Unun Sint* made his unprecedented offer to the leaders and theologians of separated Christian Churches and communions to engage in a patient and fraternal dialogue on the way in which the Roman primacy ought to be exercised, the response was probably quite disappointing to the pontiff. Probably most non-Catholic Christian leaders, as we have suggested, were themselves surprised and even taken aback by such an unexpected offer: it was not the kind of thing they thought they would ever be hearing from Rome; nor, if we think back to the days when the Catholic Church's official position on ecumenism amounted to calling for a simple return of non-Catholics to the true fold, was it the kind of message Rome was accustomed to deliver.

At first, as we have noted, apart from the mere reiterations of traditional positions that came from most of the non-Catholic religious leaders who seem to have taken any notice of the pope's encyclical at all, it almost seemed as if the major responses to the pope's initiative came only from disgruntled Catholic bishops resentful of Roman centralism and of what they considered Roman interference (which usually consisted of efforts by the Holy See to get the bishops to do what, according to Vatican II's teaching on episcopal collegiality, the bishops should have been doing on their own all along).

Here and there, however, there were some more positive responses to the pope's initiative. One of the best of them came from a French Eastern Orthodox theologian, Olivier Clément, of the Institute of St. Sergius in Paris. In 1997, two years after the encyclical, Professor Clément published a little book entitled *Rome Autrement*, which then came out in an English translation in 2003 under the title *You Are Peter*, with a foreword by the American Cardinal Avery Dulles, who characterized the book as "almost exactly the kind of response for which Pope John Paul II was hoping."

At the outset, Professor Clément recognizes that there is such a thing as a "call to unity." Throughout the book it becomes clear that he is very knowledgeable about both the history and the theology of the now millennial differences between Eastern Orthodox and Western Catholics. During the First Millennium of Christianity, he observes in an endnote, "in both East and West the faith was spoken of as 'Orthodox' and the Church as 'Catholic.'" Not a bad idea today. Moreover, his description of the nature of the Church, written from an Eastern Orthodox perspective, does not appear to differ in most of its essentials from the teaching of Vatican Council II's Dogmatic Constitution on the Church, *Lumen Gentium*. And he himself appears to recognize this fully. If his viewpoint accurately reflects Orthodox sentiment, the Second Vatican Council's great Dogmatic Constitution could thus well prove to be one of the bases upon which the terms of a reunion with the East might eventually be successfully laid out.

Above all, Professor Clément's own irenic tone and openness to consider and discuss what the real outstanding differences between the East and the West actually are would seem to indicate a distinct change of tone and attitude on the Orthodox side, and he quotes a number of other Orthodox churchmen in the same vein. All this is heartening and provides hope that further ecumenical dialogue, with good will on each side, might indeed result in further ecumenical progress, even if perhaps actual reunion cannot yet be easily foreseen.

Professor Clément recognizes, as did John Paul II in *Ut Unum Sint*, that "the problem of the papacy is clearly the greatest difficulty today, and particularly in the dialogue between Catholicism and Orthodoxy." Here both Catholics and Orthodox need to refine their thinking about just what is, and what is not, essential to the positions both sides have maintained up to now. From a Catholic point of view, it does not seem possible that Vatican Council I's assigning of a "primacy of jurisdiction" to the pope could be altered, since it represents the solemn teaching of a general council of the Church ratified by a pope. There is no higher degree of teaching than this in the Catholic Church. No pope (or council) is going to give this definition up for the simple reason that it *cannot* be given up. The key point on the Catholic side would thus seem to be, as John Paul II specified in making his original offer, to examine if there is any flexibility in how this now so firmly defined primacy can be "exercised" in order to make it more acceptable.

Olivier Clément identifies one possible avenue of further discussion when he reminds us of Pope St. Gregory the Great's understanding of the nature of the Roman primacy. John Paul II also referred back to Gregory's understanding of this in his encyclical. Gregory understood the primacy to be what he called a *principatus*. As explained by the French Catholic theologian Pierre Battifol in the 1920s, and quoted by Professor Clément:

> The *principatus* is an assistance that comes into play when someone appeals to the pope and when the pope deems his intervention opportune and necessary. The *principatus* has nothing to do with organized and imposed centralization. The reference to "appeals" here is important. As John Paul II also reminded us, papal primacy in the East during the First Millennium of Christianity was exercised mostly as a result of appeals

that came from the East. The bishops of Rome did not
normally exercise, nor did they attempt to exercise, the
same kind of direct authority that they exercised virtually from the beginning over the Churches in Italy and,
for complex historical reasons, eventually came to exercise over the whole Western Church. In the East, though,
papal authority only came into play when disputes or differences could not be resolved among the autocephalous
Churches themselves, and so an appeal had to be made
to Rome.

As Professor Clément recognizes and documents, this style of
the exercise of the primacy was long recognized in the East itself,
for example, by the (non-ecumenical) Council of Sardica (343-344),
as well as in other cases. Professor Clément also briefly discusses
— but passes over much too hurriedly, in my opinion — the case of
the famous Formula of Pope Hormisdas in the early sixth century,
when it would seem from a Western and Catholic point of view that
the Eastern Orthodox Churches formally, willingly, solemnly, and
with conviction *accepted* the Roman primacy on terms that surely
do not exceed what the Catholic Church would be obliged to require
of them today as the price of a restored unity.

The main facts of the case were these. In 519, the Byzantine
Emperor Justin I, Patriarch John of Constantinople, and a large majority of the Eastern bishops all signed and subscribed to a Formula
required by Pope Hormisdas as the price of a reunion following a
temporary schism *then*. This Formula included language affirming
the intention of "living in unity... in the Catholic religion [which]
has always been preserved without blemish in the Apostolic See."
In this Apostolic See — Rome — the Eastern bishops solemnly
agreed, "resides, whole and true, the firm foundation of the Christian religion."

Some of the language of this Formula of Hormisdas was repeated word for word in Vatican I's definition of the primacy of the

pope. By subscribing to this Formula, the Eastern bishops surely *committed their Churches* to the position they were agreeing to. If the solemn pronouncements of synodally assembled Christian bishops mean anything — as the Eastern Orthodox certainly believe they do in the case of the first seven ecumenical councils among other cases — then the formal acceptance by the Eastern Christian Churches of the Formula of Hormisdas ought to mean that the East *did* formally and officially accept the Roman primacy. From a Catholic and Western point of view, those Eastern Orthodox who today hold that the primacy has to entail something less than what the Formula specified would seem to have receded from a position once solemnly accepted and proclaimed by their Churches.

This is surely one of the questions that needs to be out on the table in any future ecumenical discussions on the subject of the Roman primacy, and there are, of course, other issues that need to be brought out and aired as well. Professor Clément speaks of the Roman primacy as having been "contaminated by the problem of power," and, in a sense, this is true, at least in some historical periods. Such measures as the appointment of a Latin patriarch of Constantinople by Pope Innocent III, as well as other similar measures that sought to "Latinize" the Eastern Church at a time when the Western Church believed it had the power to do so, were certainly illegitimate and were huge mistakes, which the Catholic Church today need not even pause in repudiating.

Pope John Paul II's many and profuse "apologies" on his various Eastern visits were surely intended to put such past errors and embarrassments behind us. During his visit to Greece in April, 2001, the pope offered a specific apology for the sacking of Constantinople by Western Crusaders during the Fourth Crusade in 1204. Such things took place long ago in a different world and *should* be put behind us. Still, Catholics today cannot just pass over them as of no importance, either; they constitute the reasons why many Eastern Orthodox still distrust the Catholic Church and want no part of the Roman primacy (that their ancestors had nevertheless once accepted!). Obviously, attitudes must be transformed on both sides; hearts as well as minds must be changed. This is precisely what the Catholic Church has been attempting to bring about since the Decree on Ecumenism, *Unitatis Redintegratio*, was promulgated at Vatican II.

With regard to the question of the "power" of the papacy, it must be recognized that the very real power struggles in which the papacy was engaged with lay rulers in medieval times were struggles that these lay rulers themselves often thrust upon the Church in seeking to control her. The papacy was generally fighting for its independence and hence for that of the Church. And it was a fight that, in medieval times, the papacy basically won in the West. This victory of the papacy in those times, though, was one in which all believers in the Niceno-Constantinopolitan Creed ought to rejoice, for it meant in very broad terms that the Church was henceforth *free* to proclaim her Creed, preach the Gospel, and administer the sacraments of Jesus Christ!

It is quite true, as Professor Clément notes, that the East and the West have had very different histories; and these very different histories have had their effects on how the faith has been proclaimed and lived in the East as well as in the West. But this basic fact does not simply somehow redound to the credit of the East (which was presumably *not* "contaminated" by "power," according to the current Eastern account). The East had and has its own problems to face, including problems having to do with the exercise of "power." It is, of course, greatly to the credit of the Eastern Orthodox Churches that they have preserved the basic faith and sacraments of Christ, often in hostile environments. They have done so in the face both of alien rule by Muslims, and by sometimes almost equally oppressive "Orthodox" governments, where the state assumed a rule over the Church that has sometimes been correctly styled "Caesaropapist." Perhaps the Orthodox churchmen of those days should have taken a leaf from the book of the popes, and resisted the rule of state power to a greater extent than they did. Clément remarks that "the East did not experience the papacy as it developed in the West.... It refused it in anticipation."

But perhaps it shouldn't have. As things turned out in history, the papacy has carried out a number of functions essential to the preservation and expansion of the faith of Jesus Christ in this world. Maybe the East should have been paying closer attention — or should perhaps begin paying closer attention today. As unfortunately sometimes appears to be the case, the Orthodox cannot simply claim the moral high ground in all of the historical developments that have resulted in the Christianity that we know today. Some of the developments in the papacy to which the Orthodox object today came about as a result of some very difficult times in the passage of the Western Church down through her particular history. Just as there has been a legitimate "development of doctrine" in the history of the Church — as so masterfully expounded by John Henry Newman in his *Essay on the Development of Christian Doctrine* — so there has been a legitimate development of Church structures and institutions as well, often in response to the vicissitudes that the Church has had to face in the course of her long history.

Beginning with the original commission to Peter at Caesarea Philippi, the institutional primacy of the pope has developed in Peter's successors in precisely this fashion. This is something the Eastern Orthodox ought to be able to understand, since institutions upon which they set such great store, such as the ancient patriarchates and the councils, were developed in a very similar fashion out of their origins in the primitive Church. The Orthodox *already* believe in the valid development of such necessary Church structures, in other words; it is just that they do not believe in the papacy as one of those valid Church structures that developed with time out of the primitive Church. As for the successive developments in the institution of the papacy, though, there was never a time when the Church in the West could simply have waited around to secure agreement with the East before proceeding on with her life and the God-given tasks assigned to her in the course of her particular history — such as summoning general councils to deal with the issues faced by the Church.

The primacy is necessary, in fact. This has been proved in the course of the Church's history, over and over again. It is hard to imagine, for example, how the Orthodox theory of a confluence or congregation of Churches headed by bishops, all equal with one another, would have fared when faced, for example, with the French Revolution and Napoleon. In that very well documented case, Pope Pius VII at one point simply abolished with the stroke of his pen the entire national hierarchy of France and created a new one. The very survival of the Catholic Church in the West probably depended upon the outcome of his action in this case. Did the pope have the authority to do what he did? What would have been done in the case of an "autocephalous" national French Church, such as Gallicanism, for example, tried but failed to establish in France?

These are questions which the Orthodox have to address and answer in the course of today's on-going ecumenical dialogue and the quest for the Christian unity for which Christ prayed. The Orthodox have to recognize, for example, that papal authority — indeed, papal "power" — developed in response to challenges that, left unchecked, would on not a few historical occasions have gravely harmed the Church and, in some cases, might even have destroyed her.

We face similar challenges in the world today. Are the Orthodox Churches prepared to face down the moral challenges posed, for example, by today's bio-technological revolution in the way that the papacy *has* been responding to those challenges? A book such as this really admirable short book, *You Are Peter*, by Olivier Clément should make Catholics realize that the Orthodox do have a serious case to make, a case which merits consideration, and, yes, "dialogue." Vatican II did right in deciding that these things have to be brought out into the open and discussed. There are good and important arguments on all sides of the vital question of Christian unity that is especially needed now in order to face the Brave New World of galloping bio-technology today, not to speak of all the other challenges faced by Christians in today's secularized world. Catholics would, of course, be greatly remiss in disregarding the kinds of arguments that Professor Clément brings forward. We *need* to try to see things as such a knowledgeable, responsible, and sincere Christian as he sees them.

At the same time, Professor Clément and other knowledgeable and sincere Eastern Orthodox Christians need to realize that, among other issues, the whole question of *authority* needs to be resolved. The nature of authority is not too clearly seen in Clément's book, any more than, in my opinion, it is completely clear in the Orthodox tradition. The Orthodox apparently believe that a decentralized authority is possible, whereas history tends to show that it is *im*possible. For authority, by its nature, is indivisible. We need think, for example, of the plaque which President Harry S. Truman is said to have kept upon his desk reading, "The buck stops here." "Passing the buck" — ducking responsibility — could no longer proceed past the locus of ultimate authority. This was an admirable expression of the true nature of authority. Authority is the power to decide, and, by its nature, it ultimately *cannot* be divided.

The Orthodox, however, apparently believe that it can be divided, for example, among the bishops of autonomous, autocephalous Churches, where no central authority obtains. But what this means is that there are some things that can never really be decided (because the buck can never really stop anywhere). The Anglican Communion seems to be currently in the process of proving this in our own day. But the problem is also illustrated by the example of the autonomous Orthodox Churches themselves, as a matter of fact, which have lacked a proper "living magisterium" once the conciliar system broke down (for them) following the seventh ecumenical council.

Christ understood the problem better when he founded his Church upon Peter and the other apostles, but, upon Peter alone, if it came down to that. Christ's wisdom in this regard has been amply reflected in the history of the Church, and, especially, of the papacy. The papacy has proved to be necessary to the Church, just as Christ saw that Peter's "primacy" was necessary in the college of the apostles.

Professor Clément appears to understand quite well that Vatican II really "solved" most of the major problems that the Orthodox have had with the Catholic Church. *Lumen Gentium* made clear, for example, that the bishops are not the "vicars" of the pope, but teach, rule, and sanctify in their own right — as the Orthodox too believe. But the bishops are not thereby any less, and necessarily, *under* the ultimate authority of the pope when decisions are required that the bishops cannot, in the nature of things, make by themselves and for each other.

Olivier Clément hopes that the papacy will return to the conception of the primacy as a "servant" of communion between the East and the West. But that, of course, is exactly what Pope John Paul II tried to do in *Ut Unum Sint*. One of the outstanding questions between the Catholic and Orthodox Churches is whether the latter will *recognize* what the pope was trying to do and respond to this initiative in kind. Let us hope that will some day turn out to be the case.

CHAPTER SIXTEEN

CONSIDERING THE PETRINE MINISTRY

A POSITIVE EVENT, which constitutes another relatively hopeful sign in response to Pope John Paul II's invitation to Church leaders and theologians to engage in "a patient and fraternal dialogue" on the subject of the Roman primacy, "leaving useless controversies behind" (UUS 96), was the symposium held on May 21-24, 2003, at the Pontifical Council for Promoting Christian Unity (PCPCU) in Rome. This symposium was organized on the basis of *Ut Unum Sint*, and was convened at the specific request of Pope John Paul II. Hosted by Cardinal Walter Kasper, president of the PCPCU, the participants, both Catholic and Orthodox, were mostly theologians and professors, although several Eastern Orthodox bishops attended as well. Eight speakers presented papers on the Petrine ministry from both Catholic and Orthodox perspectives. The proceedings were then collected into a very useful and informative book entitled: *The Petrine Ministry: Catholics and Orthodox in Dialogue*, published in 2006 by Paulist Press.

The title of the book itself is of interest. Cardinal Kasper explained at the beginning of the symposium that the terms "Petrine ministry" and "Petrine service" were being employed in place of "papal ministry" and "papacy." The reason for this change of terminology, the cardinal explained, went back to Pope John Paul II's own emphasis in the encyclical on viewing his office and function as Peter's successor as a *service*. This idea of emphasizing the pope's ministry as a service is one that has been developed fairly recently, at least in part, in response to Eastern Orthodox criticisms of how the papal office has traditionally been seen and defined and exercised in the West. This new emphasis also arose out of a wish to view and exercise the historic papal ministry more "in the light of the Gospel," Cardinal Kasper explained, "not renouncing its essential nature, but setting it in a new and wider spiritual understanding on the theoretical as well as on the practical levels."

Whether the new term, "Petrine ministry," will catch on and come into general use remains to be seen, but it seems clear that Church officials now prefer and henceforth intend to use this term. Cardinal Kasper nevertheless made clear at the beginning of the symposium that "the Catholic Church is dogmatically bound to the First and Second Vatican Councils, which she cannot give up; also the Orthodox Churches are *de facto* bound by their critique of and opposition to, these dogmas. What is the room for maneuver, then? Can there be an honest solution?"

In fact, the participants in this symposium did not claim at the end of it to have found any such "solution." There was no breakthrough. There was, however, an honest and very clarifying exchange of views on both sides by participants who hold important and influential positions in their respective Churches and can surely be taken as reflecting developing opinion within those Churches. The symposium proved to be particularly valuable because of the depth of knowledge and understanding exhibited by virtually all of the speakers on the topics they had been assigned.

As had no doubt been expected, the Eastern Orthodox speakers generally defended the traditional positions of their Churches — as did the Catholic speakers. But what cannot but strike the reader of these published proceedings positively is the courteous and objective way in which the various positions on all sides were articulated and presented. There was a welcome absence of polemics or even of any suggestion that one's interlocutor maintaining a different position was hopelessly mired "in error," and was therefore perhaps even perverse. The *et tu* character that has so often and for so long characterized Catholic and Orthodox relations was nowhere in evidence. The unhappy legacy on both sides, of course, is that these relations have been too often characterized by what can only be described, sadly, as "polemics," or something not too dissimilar, and this has been the case literally for *centuries*. One of Vatican Council II's specific major aims was to try to put the relations among separated Christians on a different footing.

By itself this Roman symposium convened by Cardinal Kasper evidenced the value of Vatican II's and John Paul II's aims to try to emphasize what unites Christians rather than what divides them. Only if the *habit* is acquired of granting that one's interlocutor in dialogue at least holds a *reasonable* position will it ever be possible to reach any eventual agreement, if indeed agreement is ultimately possible.

Moreover, only when positions are articulated and mutually conceded to be at least reasonable, can possible agreement ever seem to come any *closer*. The present writer, while obviously favoring the Catholic positions, was at least able to see and understand the Orthodox positions in a new and better light, as a result of the learned discussions that took place in the course of this symposium. I was quite heartened, in fact, to encounter knowledgeable and capable Orthodox writers espousing such positions as that "the practical challenge of unity, as well as the theological urgency behind it, favor the value of a *visible* universal leader, just as they favor a visible local leader in the person of the bishop" (emphasis added).

What possible candidate for a "visible universal leader" of Christianity can even be imagined other than the bishop of Rome? Once the desirability of such a visible universal leader has been recognized, the need to *exclude* the pope from this particular role no longer obtains with the same strength.

Or again, consider the following statement by another Orthodox theologian on the subject of the "primacy of honor" which is the most that the Orthodox, including those contributing to this book, have traditionally been willing to grant to the bishop of Rome (while emphatically excluding, of course, any "primacy of jurisdiction"). This, then, is what H.E. Professor Ioannis Zizioulas, Orthodox Metropolitan of Pergamon, found himself able to say on the subject:

> With regard to the Church, [the] description of primacy as "simple honor" seems to contradict basic canonical principles, such as the ones contained in the thirty-fourth Apostolic Canon which states that every region (presumably a metropolitan district, but by extension all forms of primacy) there *must* be a primate (*prôtos*) without whom the bishops of the district can do nothing, while he himself can do nothing without them. This seems to imply that the *primus* can even block the deliberations of the synod, if he chooses to do so, *without the rest of the bishops being able to function synodically in his absence.* It is, for example, a well-known canonical provision in the Orthodox Church that in the absence of the patriarch or during the vacancy of his throne there can be no episcopal elections or the performance of any "canonical acts." Is this a "simple honor"? It appears that this phrase is useful with regard to what it intends to exclude (jurisdictional interventions, etc.) but very misleading if taken literally. There seems, in fact, not to exist, even in the Orthodox Church, "a simple primacy of honor."

But if there is no "simple primacy of honor," even in the Orthodox Churches, then what is the status that would be accorded by them to the bishop of Rome as the *prôtos* among the bishops? It is hard to see how it could be required of any holder of primacy in Christ's Church if it doesn't even exist. Obviously, a great deal hinges upon what is meant by "simple" here. At the very least, however, this key bedrock question in the ecumenical relations between Catholics and Orthodox would seem to admit of some possible reinterpretation — and, meanwhile, John Paul II has already granted that that other key word "jurisdiction" could also be open to some re-interpretation where the East is concerned. In the light of all this, it would seem that Churches accustomed to practicing "the truth in love" (Eph 4:15) with one another might eventually come to a greater degree of understanding and agreement on the subject of the primacy than can perhaps now be foreseen.

Having read over the years a fair amount about Orthodoxy and Orthodox positions — although in no way can I claim to be a bona fide expert on these subjects! — I was also impressed with the degree to which the Orthodox participants in this symposium in Rome appeared to understand that with the passage of time such past Church structures as the Pentarchy of patriarchates — Rome, Alexandria, Antioch, Constantinople, and Jerusalem — can no longer be accorded the same importance they once had in the relations between the East and the West. It has always seemed to me to be a key to a better understanding of the papacy, and, for instance, of the continuation by the papacy of such practices as convoking general councils beyond the first seven recognized by both the Catholic and Orthodox Churches, to recognize that both doctrine *and* Church structures *develop* in the course of history. The medieval popes, for example, were often obliged to expand the scope of the authority they claimed in response to various kinds of pressures against the Church by secular rulers. Their actions were in no way a simple "power grab"; they were legitimately concerned with the true freedom of the Church.

In the same way, the popes had to go on convening the councils to which the Orthodox today object because the Church still had to be governed, whether or not the Eastern bishops were prepared to participate (they were *invited* to do so, on more than one occasion). But this did not necessarily constitute any *usurpation* of power, in my opinion, as has sometimes been charged.

Anyway, the Eastern Orthodox already do recognize the *principle* of development because they recognize that the ancient patriarchates which they have championed developed in precisely that fashion. The patriarchs of Constantinople, for example, certainly expanded the exercise of their authority in various ways over time. Surely it is legitimate in any sincere search for Christian unity to recognize that perhaps some of the features of the papacy to which others object also developed — legitimately — in much the same fashion.

On the downside, I was disappointed at the degree to which the Orthodox participants in the symposium, with near unanimity, do not recognize that the Apostle Peter enjoyed the special role as head of the apostles that Catholic teaching accords to him. Apparently the Orthodox can grant that the pope is the successor of Peter; but for them that does not mean that he holds the special leadership role among the successors of the apostles, the bishops, that the Catholic Church believes to be the case. One of the Orthodox participants at the Roman symposium, the Reverend Professor Theodore Stylianopoulous, emeritus at the Holy Cross Greek Orthodox School of Theology, in Brookline, Massachusetts, noted, pertinently, that "no Orthodox scholar has ever raised doubts about either the authenticity of the key Petrine texts of Matthew 16: 16-19, Luke 22: 31-32, and John 21:15-19 or the historical reliability of the Book of Acts" — in which Peter's prominent leadership role in the early Church is described. Nevertheless, the Orthodox apparently do not draw the same conclusions from these New Testament texts that Catholics do.

This is especially disappointing because the key Petrine New Testament texts referred to here, where Peter is designated as the Rock, where Christ predicts that he will be the one to confirm his brethren, and where he is enjoined three times to feed Christ's sheep, seem on their face to be addressed "universally," i.e., not just to the apostles present on each occasion, but to the future body of the followers of Christ. Moreover, in the case of this New Testament evidence which nobody presumably disputes — it is just a matter of what it *means* — it should also be evident that even Peter's role had to develop somewhat in the course of his own lifetime in response to the needs of his ministry, which was at first exercised in the Jerusalem and Antiochian Churches, but later, in Rome, undeniably, assumed a more universal character.

If the entire authentic tradition of Christ's Church goes back to a situation where the apostles, personally chosen and commissioned by Christ, in due course handed on the powers given to them by the same Christ to their successors, the bishops, then it seems hard to deny that the first apostle among them, Peter, would also, naturally and inevitably, have also handed on the special powers granted to *him* to the bishops of Rome. The parallelism of Matthew 18:18, where all the apostles together are given the power to bind and loose, and Matthew 16:19, where Peter is separately and alone given the power to bind and loose, in fact strongly suggests this interpretation, it would seem.

And as far as the position of Rome in the post-apostolic Church is concerned, it should not be forgotten that the Apostle Paul, who, on the evidence of numerous New Testament texts, clearly himself founded Churches and appointed bishops and presbyters — the great Apostle Paul also ended his days in Rome and presumably then "handed on" *his* legacy there, as all of the apostles are supposed to have done. Given the supreme importance of Peter and Paul in the early Church, the pre-eminent position of the bishops of Rome can hardly be gainsaid. From a Catholic viewpoint, it seems almost a quibble to insist that all of the bishops who succeeded the apostles were nevertheless "equal." It does not seem that all the apostles *were* exactly equal.

Another one of the Orthodox participants in the symposium, however, the Reverend Professor Nicolae Durã, of the Romanian Orthodox Church's Bucharest Faculty of Theology, while recognizing that Peter did have a special charge from the Lord, nevertheless concludes that there is no evidence of "primacy," since no such thing is recognized in the canonical legislation of the first millennium. Yet "legislation" of this kind generally came only in response to need, for instance when a Church position or claim was challenged in various ways. There is no doubt or dispute that Rome was widely and consistently recognized during the first millennium, including in the East, as the "first" of the Churches, and "appeals" were certainly directed to the bishop of Rome, even from the East. But the need for concrete legislation spelling out the particular jurisdiction entailed in this character of being "first" and also being the recipient of various appeals did not necessarily arise. It may well not have arisen precisely *because* Rome did not generally claim to exercise any direct rule over the Churches in the East in the way that she was increasingly exercising it in the West.

These are just a couple of the questions that occur to a reader of *The Petrine Ministry.* Other questions could be raised. All in all, the book provides a very thorough and interesting overview of the current relationship between the Catholic and Eastern Orthodox Churches. A number of the issues discussed here could surely be pursued with profit, and no doubt will be so pursued, in the course of the on-going Catholic-Orthodox dialogue that continues to move ahead.

However, Christian reunion as such is not likely to emerge from a symposium such as this, no matter how positive and heartening it may be in other ways. Moreover, it seems likely that the "large views" evidenced here by these learned scholars are not necessarily as widely shared in their respective ecclesial communities. Discussion and dialogue will no doubt have to be carried on for a good while before the knowledge and attitudes found here encounter widespread acceptance within the larger Christian communities. Nevertheless, a symposium of this kind — which would probably not have been even remotely likely before Vatican Council II — represents a distinctly hopeful sign. Its focus, precisely, on the Petrine ministry indicates an awareness, on both the Catholic and Orthodox sides, of the central importance in their ecumenical relations of the question of the primacy (which John Paul II also had so presciently seen in *Ut Unum Sint*). We ourselves will have to pursue this question of the primacy yet further in subsequent chapters if we are really to do justice to the subject in the present ecumenical climate. To conclude this chapter, meanwhile, we shall quote from a remarkable contribution by one of the Catholic participants in the symposium, German theologian Hermann J. Pottmeyer, who explains in illuminating detail exactly what it was that Vatican Council I really decided when it accorded a "primacy of jurisdiction" in Christ's Church to the bishop of Rome — a primacy carried over and reaffirmed in a wider context by Vatican Council II.

It is this same "primacy of jurisdiction" which seems to be what the Eastern Orthodox object most strongly to in the Catholic position, and, indeed, often seem to fear. In his contribution, however, Hermann Pottmeyer explains how the Vatican I definitions were primarily intended to eliminate the dominance of the state over the Church (e.g., as in the case of Gallicanism in France or Josephism in Austria). The primary aim was *not* to establish a Roman "hegemony" over the whole Church. "The dogmatization of the papal primacy as sovereignty," Pottmeyer writes, "was at the heart of the Ultramontane strategy in the battle for the freedom of the Church."

Yet no less than the Eastern Orthodox today, many of the "minority" Catholic bishops at Vatican I feared that the papal jurisdiction, as the Council was preparing to define it, "appeared to be a rival jurisdiction which superseded the equally ordinary, immediate, and episcopal power of the bishop within his diocese." Pottmeyer summarizes the reply of the Vatican I conciliar commission in response to this fear in a way that would seem to make it an important if not equally valid response to the current Eastern Orthodox objections to the idea and exercise of the pope's primacy of jurisdiction. This is what he says:

• The Church is... not an absolute monarchy under the pope. The primacy has to observe the divine constitution of the Church, including the authority of the college of bishops and the individual bishops, and it must take as its guiding principle the welfare of the Church which it is to serve. All of that is assumed to be taken for granted and is not a subject for debate. The sole issue here is the question whether there is any human authority beside or above the pope which can limit his authority. This is precisely what is to be excluded.

• It is true that the full and supreme jurisdictional power of the Church exists in a twofold manner. On the one hand it pertains to the college of bishops with its head, the bishop of Rome, and also to the bishop of Rome as the visible head of the Church, independently of his acting together with the other bishops. For Christ's commission was given both to all the apostles together with Peter, and to Peter alone. This twofold structure becomes problematic only when the two forms, which are bound together by the same apostolic commission and the same sacrament, are considered as separate powers competing with one another, as they are regarded by conciliarism and Gallicanism.

• The definition of papal jurisdiction as "ordinary" power does not mean that it should be considered normal for the pope constantly to intervene in the dioceses. Rather, the word "ordinary" is used as the opposite of "delegated" and means: the primacy is grounded not in a delegation by the Church, but in Christ's commission to Peter.

• It is designated as "immediate" power because the pope — if the *necessitas ecclesiae* demands — can intervene everywhere within the Church, directly and without mediation or permission by any other authority.

• The designation as "truly episcopal" power is intended to counter the Gallican error that the pope infringes the sacramentally transmitted rights reserved for the responsible bishop when he intervenes in a diocese. The pastoral power of the pope and the bishops is based on the same sacrament, the only difference being that the pope is endowed with the *episcope* for the entire Church and in its supreme form, while that of the bishops is valid only for their diocese and in hierarchical subordination beneath the pope.

It is unfortunate that the primacy of the pope over the whole Church, as defined by Vatican Council I, has not normally been explained or understood as well as it is so clearly and admirably summarized here by the Reverend Professor Hermann J. Pottmeyer. No doubt there is much that the Eastern Orthodox would still object to even as it is so plainly and unmistakably laid out. However, there is great merit in stating the case as clearly as possible; for as stated here, the primacy would seem to bear little resemblance to the primacy so often assailed in so many typical past polemics on the subject.

CHAPTER SEVENTEEN

FIVE ORTHODOX THEOLOGIANS
EXAMINE THE PRIMACY;
THE CDF CLARIFIES THE ISSUES

IT SHOULD HAVE BECOME increasingly clear from what we have covered up to now that the doctrine of the primacy of the pope is the key Catholic doctrine on which some kind of agreement will have to be reached before any true Christian reunion is possible (or perhaps even conceivable). In an address to the Vatican Secretariat for Promoting Christian Unity as far back as April 28, 1968, Pope Paul VI stated: "The pope, as we well know, is undoubtedly the gravest obstacle in the path of ecumenism."

A year later, on June 10, 1969, the same Pope addressed the World Council of Churches at its headquarters in Geneva, beginning his discourse by announcing: "Our name is Peter." Making reference to the New Testament, he interpreted Peter's role as a "fisher of men" (Mt 4:19; Mk 1:17) and as a "shepherd" (Jn 21: 15-17); and he spoke very plainly to his WCC auditors, as follows:

> The Lord has given us a ministry of communion. He has given us this charism, certainly not to isolate us from you or to exclude understanding, fellowship, and, ultimately, the re-composition of unity among us (*The Pope Speaks*, 14, 1969, pp. 150-153).

Fifteen years later, Pope John Paul II went to Geneva and addressed the same World Council of Churches in his turn. He recalled his predecessor's earlier visit, when the latter had asked for forgiveness for any wrongs against separated brethren committed on the Catholic side — a practice which Pope John Paul II practically institutionalized during his long pontificate. Nevertheless, John Paul II made clear the Catholic Church's continuing belief that his office was "the visible pole and guarantee of unity in full fidelity to the apostolic tradition and to the faith of the fathers.... To be in communion with the bishop of Rome is to give visible evidence that one is in communion with all who confess that same faith, with those who have confessed it since Pentecost, and with those who will confess it until the day of the Lord shall come" (*Origins*, June 28, 1984).

In order to be in (or return to) communion with the bishop of Rome, however, it is obviously necessary to recognize the unique position in the Church founded by Christ of the bishops of that see, the successors of the head Apostle Peter. The question of the primacy of the pope thus inescapably keeps recurring, and for those Christians who do not accept it, it surely does constitute the "obstacle" to reunion which Pope Paul VI said it did. Some observers have even noted the great irony inherent in the fact that, while the pope is "the visible pole and guarantee of unity," as John Paul II insisted, he is at the same time "the gravest obstacle in the path of ecumenism," as Paul VI pointed out. The record of the dialogue contained in *The Petrine Ministry*, which we looked at in the previous chapter, is thus squarely focused on the essential question, even if today's ecumenical dialogue partners, including those representing the Catholic Church, have for the most part up to this time tended to avoid the specific question of the primacy, preferring to deal with subjects on which the possibility of reaching agreement were thought to be greater.

It is not the case, however, that no one has wished or has attempted to deal with the question of the primacy at all. On the contrary, as far back as 1960, even before the Second Vatican Council got underway, a group of distinguished Eastern Orthodox theologians who later attended the Council as observers — Nicholas Afanassieff, Nicholas Koulomzine, John Meyendorff, and Alexander Schmemann — published a book entitled, precisely, *The Primacy of Peter* (edited by John Meyendorff). The book was originally written in French; an English translation came out in 1963, while the Council was still going on in Rome. That the book is still considered on the Orthodox side to be something of an authoritative statement on the subject may perhaps be gauged by the fact that St. Vladimir's Seminary Press in Crestwood, New York, reprinted the book in 1992 with an additional chapter by Veselin Kesich. It remains in print, and is favorably cited by some of the Orthodox contributors to *The Petrine Ministry.*

While the Orthodox authors of *The Primacy of Peter* themselves make no claim to provide a complete account of the Orthodox position on the primacy — nor could anything resembling a complete account be essayed in a brief compass in any case — the issues discussed by these authors do at least provide good snapshots of the major questions surrounding the primacy that pertain to today's Catholic-Orthodox ecumenical dialogue.

The first of the essays in *The Primacy of Peter* is by Nicholas Koulomzine, who very competently reviews the place of the Apostle Peter in the primitive Church. The second essay, by Veselin Kesich, written many years later, really elaborates on pretty much the same subject but with specific reference to whether Peter himself ever exercised anything properly described as a headship or "primacy" among the apostles. Neither Koulomzine nor Kesich ignores or passes over the relevant scriptural texts and other evidence concerning the position of Peter in the early Church, and both authors readily affirm, on the evidence of the New Testament texts, that Peter was indisputably the "first" among the apostles. Indeed, the position of being "first" (*protos*) appears to be a perennial favorite topic for these, and perhaps for other, Orthodox theologians. The implication for most of them, though, is that while the pope might well be considered "first" among the bishops of the Church, the strong Eastern Orthodox tradition seems to be that this would mean merely that he was the "first among equals," or *primus inter pares*, as they are accustomed to say.

But being "first" in this fashion is, for these Orthodox theologians, a far cry from exercising any "primacy of jurisdiction," according to current Orthodox theory. They do not concede that the Apostle Peter exercised anything like "jurisdiction" or provided authoritative direction that was mandatory for the early Church; in their view, he was in no way "over" his fellow apostles, but merely the "first" among them. They presumably do not believe, in other words, that Peter issued, or could issue, "orders," which the other apostles were then obliged to "obey."

It is no doubt true enough that the New Testament accounts, although they certainly do consistently portray Peter as the first among the apostles, and, indeed, as the "head" of them, do not really otherwise discuss the matter in these particular terms — perhaps because the problem as we see it did not arise in the early Church. Catholics see the headship of Peter as described in the New Testament as strongly, if not decisively, supportive of the position of the pope's subsequent headship of the Catholic Church, while the Orthodox deny that the New Testament evidence proves any such thing.

However that may be, the Orthodox today believe they are justified in interpreting this New Testament evidence in accordance with their own ecclesiological views (as, of course, the Catholics do too!). And if for the Orthodox Peter did not exercise any "supervisory" authority over the other apostles, then they do not see how the successors of Peter in the see of Rome can claim to exercise any such authority over the other bishops of the Church either.

In any case, both of these first two Orthodox authors in *The Primacy of Peter* also agree that whatever authority, if any, Peter may have exercised over the other apostles, he was unable to hand it on to his successors. They do not ignore or discount Christ's three famous Petrine charges, of which we have already taken note more than once in these pages; but, once again, they simply do not draw from these passages the same conclusions that the Catholic Church has traditionally drawn from them. They deny that either the New Testament or any other evidence from the early Church proves that Peter had powers over the other apostles that he was able to pass on to the bishops of Rome. It thus does not seem that these famous proof-texts, vital for Catholics, are really usable at all in the on-going Catholic-Orthodox ecumenical dialogue. If the Orthodox should ever come to agree in some other way to a Roman primacy, then perhaps they might begin to grant some probative status to these Gospel passages as well; but it seems quite unlikely at this point that they will ever accept any kind of Roman primacy *because* of them.

John Meyendorff, a long-time professor at St. Vladimir's Seminary, reviews the whole question of Peter in Byzantine theology. Again, his treatment is competently and positively presented. He writes in a manner much more calm and irenic than was apparently the case for some if not much of that same Byzantine theology down through the centuries, when sharp exchanges, if not actual polemics, were only too likely to occur in what then passed for "dialogue." Though he may have eschewed polemics, however, the Reverend Professor Meyendorff nevertheless concludes that for the Byzantines, "the succession of Peter depends upon confession of the true faith." But if that is true, then what other Church has a better record than — or even remotely comparable to — the Church of Rome in affirming the true faith?

This question is never answered; indeed, it is not even raised in the way that Catholics would raise it. Rather, this distinguished Orthodox theologian simply reiterates a position greatly favored in his tradition which, perhaps curiously and certainly ironically, the Orthodox trace back to a Western Father, St. Cyprian of Carthage. The position is that *all* of the bishops of the Church are "successors of Peter." Peter stood for *all* of the bishops of the Church when he was given his famous charge by Christ.

Another contributor to this Orthodox volume, *The Primacy of*

Peter, is the late Nicholas Afanassieff (d. 1966), who taught at the Orthodox Theological Institute in Paris. He contrasts the respective Catholic and Orthodox positions on the primacy by distinguishing two distinct types of ecclesiology, a "universal ecclesiology," which he says is favored by Rome, and a "Eucharistic ecclesiology," which he thinks is characteristic of the Orthodox Churches. "Wherever the Eucharist is, there is the Church," he writes. For him each local Church is complete and "catholic" by virtue of its valid Eucharist. This approach to ecclesiology yields a totality of "equal" local Churches, each complete in itself, with no need for any "primacy" over them by any one Church. Afanassieff denies that there ever was any "universal" primacy in the early Church, and he considers the idea of such a primacy as it developed in the West to be a strictly juridical notion, superseding and obscuring the evangelical idea of grace.

For the Catholic, this kind of scheme seems to possess no way for the local churches to be necessarily linked together as the one universal Church to which even Christ made specific reference (cf. Mt 16:18). Yet, though it seems deficient, this kind of approach by Afanassieff and other Orthodox thinkers has nevertheless had enormous influence in the West among Catholic theologians not content with the Church's traditional "universal ecclesiology," which does in some ways seem to represent a largely juridical-type approach. The Afanassieff "Eucharistic" approach, in fact, contributed greatly to the new "ecclesiology of communion" that was enshrined in Vatican II's Dogmatic Constitution on the Church, *Lumen Gentium*. One of the Council's explicit aims in developing this "ecclesiology of communion" was to facilitate greater rapprochement with the Eastern Orthodox.

The final contribution to *The Primacy of Peter* was Alexander Schmemann (d. 1983), who also taught at St. Vladimir's Seminary. While not departing from the Orthodox position, his contribution seems more open to the idea, and perhaps even to the necessity, of a primacy in Christ's Church. He is, in fact, quite critical of the

Orthodox tradition, both with regard to the allowing of state power over the Church and to the fact that the Orthodox way has resulted in "national" Churches, technically in communion with each other, but often scarcely interacting with each other. He appeals to his fellow Orthodox to cast off what he calls "an age-long, anti-Roman prejudice," which, in his view, is what has mostly led the Orthodox to deny the primacy. He writes in this connection:

> At a relatively recent date there arose among the Orthodox Churches the opinion that the Church is based in her life on the principle of autocephaly.... According to this position, the principle of autocephaly is not only one of the historical expressions of her universal structure, but precisely the ecclesiological foundation of the Church and her life. In other words, the unique universal organism of Roman ecclesiology is opposed here to autocephalous organisms, each one constituted by several dioceses.... All these autocephalies are absolutely equal among themselves, and this equality excludes any universal center of primacy.

Schmemann concludes that "having rejected and still rejecting it [i.e., the universal primacy] in its Roman form, i.e., as universal power, the Orthodox conscience has easily accepted it in the so-called autocephalies...."

This position of Alexander Schmemann's would seem to be one on which a positive ecumenical dialogue on the primacy might well go forward with some prospect of bearing fruit. However that may be, the overall testimony of the Orthodox-authored *Primacy of Peter* suggests that the Catholic and Orthodox positions on the subject are still quite far apart. Further dialogue concerning the primacy will surely continue to encounter difficulties and disagreements, and it is not easy to see at the present time how these can be resolved or cleared away. And if the primacy poses this kind of difficulty for the Eastern Orthodox, who believe in and recognize both sacramentality and definite Church authority, it is not hard to see how much more difficult it is likely to be for non-Catholic Christian Churches and communions with hierarchical, sacerdotal, and sacramental systems that are much less complete than those of the Eastern Orthodox.

It might well be, indeed, that the issue of the primacy could continue to prove to be intractable to the point where true Christian reunion will not be possible at all in any foreseeable future, in spite of sincere good will and continuing expressions of a desire for it on all sides. Such an outcome would be contrary both to the sincere efforts and convictions of Vatican II and of the recent popes, of course; it would also be plainly contrary to the prayer of Jesus Christ himself. Can serious believers in Jesus justify what amounts to rejection of his prayer because they do not like the pope or fail to see how the pope serves Christ's Gospel in this world? In some ways, of course, and for obvious reasons, the pope is already widely accepted as the principal "leader" of world Christianity, but is this all that can be said for him? Is it possible that he may not be able to get beyond this status of simple world leader in the eyes of many non-Catholic Christians simply because the latter cannot find any way to the acceptance of his formal primacy?

Precisely because the primacy of the pope remains such an important issue, then, the Holy See, following Pope John Paul II's invitation to the other Churches and Christian communities in *Ut Unum Sint* to join with him in reflecting further on the issue of the primacy and its exercise, decided to issue another key document summarizing what it called "the essential points of Catholic doctrine on the primacy." Entitled "Reflections on the Primacy of the Successor of Peter in the Mystery of the Church," it was published on October 30, 1998, by the Congregation for the Doctrine of the Faith. It was signed by Cardinal Joseph Ratzinger, then prefect of the CDF, but now, of course, Pope Benedict XVI, and by Archbishop Tarcisio Bertone, then CDF secretary, but now the Cardinal Secretary of State in the Vatican. These CDF "Reflections" followed upon a symposium on the primacy sponsored in Rome by the Congregation in 1996 — that is, shortly after the pope had issued his 1995 "invitation" to dialogue.

This important but still too largely neglected CDF document unambiguously declares that "the ministry of unity entrusted to Peter belongs to the permanent structure of Christ's Church." The document properly grants that the bishop of Rome is a member of the college of bishops and that the world's "bishops are his brothers in the ministry." However, "episcopal collegiality does not stand in opposition to the [pope's] personal exercise of the primacy nor should it relativize it." Primacy and collegiality exist together. It goes on to point out, moreover, that papal primacy differs drastically "from the offices of governance found in human societies: It is not an office of coordination or management, nor can it be reduced to a primacy of honor or be conceived as a political monarchy."

The primacy belongs, in fact, to a unique system which was founded by none other than Jesus Christ himself upon the apostles. The apostles, in their turn, handed on the powers given to them by Christ to their successors, the bishops of the Church. The bishops possess what in ecclesial language is called immediate and ordinary power to teach, rule, and sanctify (administer the sacraments) in the Church (diocese) over which they are placed. Any comparison of this structure with secular power structures, especially those common today, is bound to be inexact. For example, Catholic bishops exercise what we today call executive, legislative, and judicial power all rolled into one. Yet the bishops are not exactly "monarchs," either; they do not operate by asserting any kind of "royal will," but are bound by the tradition and canon law of the Church. The Church's system is indeed unique. And all the bishops together do constitute a "college," as Vatican II emphasized, and as the Eastern Orthodox would seem to agree. All of the bishops have the *same* immediate and ordinary power over the Church (diocese) entrusted to them.

However, there is one other unique feature in this already unique system established, as we have noted, by Jesus Christ himself: *one bishop* only in the college of bishops, namely, the bishop of Rome, is the successor of the Apostle Peter, the pope. The pope possesses in full *over the whole Church* the same immediate and ordinary power that each bishop has over his own diocese. At the same time this full, supreme, and universal power of the pope over the whole Church does not supersede or diminish or nullify the power of the bishop in his own diocese; the latter is what normally obtains and is exercised on behalf of the faithful by each bishop.

But there is one condition on the bishop's exercise of his immediate and ordinary power, however: it must be exercised with the permission of the bishop of Rome. Meanwhile, the pope's special power runs concurrently with that of the bishops of the world and comes into play at any given time or place as deemed necessary by the pope himself. The pope normally leaves the running of the Church to the bishops but is *obliged* to intervene to preserve the integrity of the faith; that is the purpose for which he possesses his *universal* immediate and ordinary power. The record of the popes down through history shows that they *have* constantly done this, often in situations where after the fact it is hard to see how the faith could possibly have been preserved otherwise.

This is what "the primacy of the pope" is ultimately all about, then: the preservation of the integrity of the faith, of the message Jesus delivered to his apostles. Jesus made this plain in his various charges to Peter. This is what other Christians will ultimately have to come to terms with if they truly desire the unity which they so often say they do desire. Moreover, the nature of the mission and the power possessed by the pope is not something any current incumbent of Peter's chair can do anything about; it is what it is; not even — or especially! — the pope can change it. Though it is full, supreme, and ordinary, the pope's power is *not* absolute, by the way, nor is it in any way arbitrary. Rather, it is quite severely limited and circumscribed. The popes are *bound*, for example, by the formal acts of their hundreds of predecessors. They *cannot* change or reverse what their predecessors have definitively decided and promulgated.

Pope John Paul II, with evident sincerity, invited other Christian leaders to dialogue with him concerning the proper exercise of his power, but the power itself is something that was given to Peter by Christ and has been passed on to Peter's successors, the popes. Neither John Paul II, nor any other pope, could change that fact even if he wanted to.

Much more could be said on this subject than the brief summary that we have been able to essay here. A much more elaborate and detailed description of all this can be found, for example, in Vatican Council II's Dogmatic Constitution on the Church, *Lumen Gentium*, especially its Chapter III.

Because the primacy itself is of such great importance, however, for ecumenical dialogue as well as in other ways, the Congregation for the Doctrine of the Faith's 1998 "Reflections on the Primacy of the Successor of Peter" now constitutes an important and perhaps even indispensable supplement to *Lumen Gentium*. It lays out exactly what will have to be discussed and settled with dialogue partners who may well be as knowledgeable and sophisticated on the subject as the Eastern Orthodox authors in their book, *The Primacy of Peter,* proved to be — or as Olivier Clément, in his book, *You Are Peter,* proved to be. The CDF document similarly sets the proper limits on what representatives of the Catholic Church engaged in dialogue are obliged to hold and uphold. The preparation and issuance of these CDF "Reflections" probably became strictly necessary once John Paul II had issued his invitation for serious dialogue on the primacy.

These CDF "Reflections," finally, specify that "there is no other authority to which the Roman pontiff must juridically answer for his exercise of the gift he has received.... This does not mean, however, that the pope has absolute power. Listening to what the Churches are saying is, in fact, an earmark of the ministry of unity."

These same "Reflections on the Primacy of the Successor of Peter," though, were not the only study conducted by this Roman Congregation under the headship of the future Pope Benedict XVI on vital topics related to ecumenism. On May 28, 1992, the CDF also sent a Letter to the Bishops of the Catholic Church on "Some Aspects of the Church Understood as Communion" (with the Latin title *Communionis Notio*) clarifying the concept of the new "ecclesiology of communion" which figures so prominently in both *Lumen Gentium* and *Unitatis Redintegratio*. This CDF Letter *Communionis Notio* addresses among other things the claim in the influential "Eucharistic ecclesiology" developed by Nicholas Affanassieff and others that "where the Eucharist is celebrated, the totality of the mystery of the Church would be made present in such a way as to render any other principle of unity or universality inessential."

On the contrary, as this CDF Letter specifies: "... the oneness and indivisibility of the Eucharistic body of the Lord implies the oneness of his mystical body, which is the one and indivisible Church. From the Eucharistic center arises the necessary openness of every celebrating community, of every particular Church. By allowing itself to be drawn into the open arms of the Lord, it achieves insertion into his one and undivided body. For this reason too, the existence of the Petrine ministry, which is a foundation of the unity of the episcopate and of the universal Church, bears a profound correspondence to the Eucharistic character of the Church" (CN 11).

CHAPTER EIGHTEEN

A CATHOLIC CONVERT FROM ORTHODOXY MAKES HIS CASE

EVEN THOUGH THE QUESTION of the primacy of the pope may be the most important question involved in ecumenical dialogue today, it is still far from being the only question. This is true as regards all of the dialogue partners with which the Catholic Church is currently engaged in ecumenical discussions. Once again, though, it is especially true in the case of the ongoing dialogue with the Eastern Orthodox Churches. While a renewed positive and cordial spirit appears now to reign again in the Joint International Commission for Theological Dialogue between the Orthodox Church and the Catholic Church, after a five-year period during which talks were broken off, positions long maintained and even hardened, as well as the actual prejudices (on both sides) of nearly a millennium, still need to be re-examined and re-considered in the light of today's new ecumenical principles and attitudes. The new ecumenism in no way comes about automatically.

There are "traditionalists" on both sides, for example, who still think that even to talk about ecumenism is "heretical." Moreover, not a few Catholics have simply tuned the new ecumenism out as of little real interest, and, as the validating proof of their attitude, they point to the fact that no reunion has been achieved in spite of all the efforts since Vatican II more than forty years ago. Nor does any such reunion even remotely appear to be in the offing. On the other side,

meanwhile, as recently as February, 2007, a newly elected Bulgarian Orthodox bishop declared on his country's TV — and the story
was picked up by the world media — that "the pope is a heretic." —
that "the Orthodox canons make him a heretic."

Clearly, new attitudes and outlooks imperatively must be developed. That, in fact, is what the popes since Vatican II have been
steadily trying to foster. If this new openness of theirs is actually
leading to a comparable process of re-examination on the Orthodox
side — which does seem slowly, if still sometimes rather hesitantly,
to be occurring, at least in some Orthodox countries (and is spite
of the example of the new Bulgarian Orthodox bishop just quoted!)
— then future Christian generations might well look back on some
of today's initiatives as the beginnings of a real and true process
of reunion between the Catholic Church and the Eastern Orthodox
Churches.

For the present, however, there is no getting around the fact
that any such reunion is surely still a long way off (as we have abundantly seen in these pages already). Many outstanding and unresolved differences continue to prevent any such reunion from taking place in the near future. The difficult task of examining and
evaluating these outstanding differences, especially the theological
and doctrinal differences, although some progress has been made, is
really not yet very far beyond its first beginnings. In one important
sense, though, it is surely necessary to lay out these differences with
absolute clarity *in order to be able to engage in any realistic discussion of them* that might lead to overcoming them. And this is where
two books written by Catholic author James Likoudis come in.

James Likoudis is quite well known in the American Catholic
world as a noted writer and speaker, as well as a long-time officer,
and later president, of Catholics United for the Faith (from which
he is now retired). He himself is a convert from Eastern Orthodoxy
of many years standing, and over the years he has maintained a
vital, indeed a passionate, interest in the prospects for reunion between the Eastern and Western Churches. He is very well versed in

both the Catholic and the Orthodox theological literature, and at the same time he is wholly faithful to the judgments of the Magisterium of the Catholic Church. His knowledge of Eastern Orthodox writers may very well be unequaled among contemporary Catholic writers and observers dealing with Eastern Orthodoxy. (In the interests of full disclosure, I must mention that I personally worked with him as a colleague for a number of years, and he is, of course, a friend. We co-authored together in 1981 the book, *The Pope, the Council, and the Mass*, a revised, updated edition of which was published in 2006 by Emmaus Road Publishing.)

In the main, the work for which James Likoudis has been best known up to now has not been his work on Eastern Orthodoxy. Rather, he has been very strongly focused on the problems of the Catholic Church in the post-conciliar era, and has written and spoken mainly on such subjects as catechetics, sex education, liturgy, and the like. He has thus not generally moved in what we might term ecumenical circles; nor has he taken part in the "official" dialogues that have been going on between Catholics and Eastern Orthodox since the end of Vatican II. Nevertheless, he has published two books which, together, practically constitute a thorough short course on all the outstanding issues, theological and otherwise, that have predominated in the course of the schism between the East and the West that has now endured for nearly a thousand years. The two books in question are: *The Divine Primacy of the Bishop of Rome and Modern Eastern Orthodoxy* (2002) and *Eastern Orthodoxy and the See of Peter* (2006). Both of these books are available from the author himself at P.O. Box 852, Montour Falls, New York 14865.

These two books are strongly recommended to any reader who wishes to know what the real, substantive doctrinal, theological, and historical differences are that have continued to prevent the consummation of any Church reunion between East and West up to now. In spite of all the good will, as well as all the cordial words, which Catholic and Orthodox leaders now regularly employ with and towards each other, the reunion that nearly everybody

says should take place still does *not* take place. The differences between the Churches still remain unresolved and have to be worked
through. Stressing what is already agreed upon may have gotten the
ecumenical dialogue going, but eventually — usually very soon —
the dialogue always comes up against the hard reality of the differences that do persist.

James Likoudis is not greatly concerned with what we might
call the "politics" of ecumenism, notably the now quite regular exchanges between Church leaders and the like. Although he is aware
of such things, as well as of the successive documents being produced in the course of the ongoing dialogues, his focus is on the
bed-rock historical and doctrinal differences between Catholics and
the Orthodox which have prevented reunion up to now, and which
continue to prevent it. Both of his books stress and discuss the outstanding doctrinal and historical differences that persist. *The Divine
Primacy of the Bishop of Rome and Modern Eastern Orthodoxy* is
cast in the form of letters to a Greek Orthodox correspondent named
Euthymios. It is an expanded version of an earlier and somewhat
slimmer book with the same title that the author published in 1999;
this earlier version consisted of a vigorous response to a book written by a British author who had converted from Catholicism to Eastern Orthodoxy. Likoudis was easily able to show from the relevant
documents that this British author's treatment of the "defects" of the
Catholic position vis-á-vis the claims of Eastern Orthodoxy was not
very convincing in the light of all the relevant facts.

All the material from this earlier 1999 version of the *Divine
Primacy* was then incorporated into the present 2002 version, and
much was added. Evidently much of the added material was inspired
by actual letters received by the author as a result of publishing the
earlier version, and thus the text enjoys the immediacy of actual
debate. By and large, Likoudis answers the queries of his Greek
Orthodox correspondent completely and well. The main questions
outstanding between the two communions are pretty well all covered, beginning with the original schism of 1054, which the author

shows was not a definitive break, but was part of a much longer process of gradual and increasing estrangement between the East and the West. In a couple of letters, in fact, Likoudis doubles back to the earlier so-called "Photian Schism" of the ninth century.

In the same epistolary form, the author covers both the historical questions from the Council of Florence (1431-35) on, and the doctrinal ones, such as the famous *Filioque* ("and the Son") clause in the Nicene Creed, which Likoudis shows need not be an insuperable obstacle to reunion. Indeed, as he notes, some Eastern Orthodox theologians have actually conceded this point. At the same time, it is not even clear that the clause itself needs to be retained in the Creed itself, if maintaining the Creed's wording exactly as it issued from the Councils of Nicaea and Constantinople in the fourth century would move us closer to reunion. Surely there can be nothing intrinsically *wrong* with maintaining the Creed as it was originally formulated and issued at these first two famous ecumenical councils of the Church accepted in both East and West.

What the *Filioque* clause, which was added later to the Creed in the West — Pope Benedict VIII approved the addition of the clause in 1014 — expresses, of course, is a legitimate *development of doctrine.* The Orthodox Churches, as far as one can see, have still not worked out for themselves a complete theology of the development of doctrine, and this is surely one of the reasons why they continue to consider various Western developments to be illegitimate. This whole question is in need of further, honest joint examination. What is to be hoped might emerge from the ongoing ecumenical dialogue is, precisely, a greater understanding and acceptance on the part of the Orthodox about how doctrines and practices do "develop" legitimately in the history of the Church.

The phenomenon is not unknown in their own tradition, as a matter of fact. They recognize it in the case of, e.g., the ancient patriarchates, which certainly did not exist in the primitive Church. But what they do not recognize as legitimate are some of the developments in the West which took place after the separation, and which grew out of the same kinds of ecclesiastical necessities as development such as that of the patriarchates earlier that they do recognize.

In the case of the *Filioque* clause, of course, the *truth* of the doctrine it affirms would have to continue to be affirmed and protected in some other way by the Church if the clause itself were dropped from the Creed. However, as James Likoudis notes, solid Catholic theologians such as Fathers Yves Congar and Louis Bouyer have stated that there is no *a priori* reason why the *Filioque* clause needs to be retained in the Creed itself; not everything that the Church believes and teaches, even infallibly, *is* in the Creed. Apparently the Holy See already allows the Creed in Greek to be professed without its inclusion. More than that, it may be of some significance that the recent document which the Congregation for the Doctrine of the Faith issued on June 30, 2000, *Dominus Iesus* — and which we shall examine in the next chapter — reproduces the original Niceno-Constantinopolitan Creed *without* the *Filioque* clause! This CDF document aroused no little controversy when it first came out — and was regarded by many Protestants and others, including some liberal Catholic theologians, as being excessively "hard line" and *anti*-ecumenical in its insistence on restating, plainly and without ambiguity, a number of sometimes controverted Catholic doctrines such as that the fullness of Christ's grace and truth are to be found in the Catholic Church alone.

As with the *Filioque* clause question, so with the question of the pope's primacy of jurisdiction over the whole Church: this latter question, as we have already seen, remains the major doctrinal question that the Orthodox Churches do not accept. On this topic, James Likoudis treats his Orthodox interlocutor, Euthymios, to one of the most thorough and cogent explanations of the history and theology of the primacy to be found anywhere. More than half of the 52 letters to Euthymios which make up the book deal directly with the question of the primacy. As the author does not fail to explain, the Orthodox idea is that the primates of the fourteen or so separate national Orthodox Churches which make up the "Orthodox Church" are all "equal," with only a primacy of honor accorded to the Ecumenical Patriarch of Constantinople — as, in theory, the bishop of Rome, the pope, is conceded by many Orthodox to be *primus inter pares*. But, as we have already noted, this Orthodox idea of the episcopate fails to reflect the model of the original apostolic college since there is no "Peter" at the head of it.

Many Orthodox regularly make the claim that they alone have handed down the apostolic faith and practice intact and unchanged, with no inadmissible additions such as those supposedly added in the West; yet the Orthodox *do* omit, precisely, the role of any successor of Peter at the head of the college of bishops. Hence they have evidently *not quite* handed down the apostolic faith and practice intact and unchanged!

The other book by James Likoudis, *Eastern Orthodoxy and the See of Peter*, published in 2006, is a collection of periodical articles published by the author. While it covers some of the same territory as the previous book, all of the chapters are eminently worth reading and throw new light on the outstanding issues. One chapter in particular that is simply vital in this volume is the chapter entitled "Contraception and Eastern Orthodoxy: *Humanae Vitae* as Touchstone of the True Faith." The reference here, of course, is to Pope Paul VI's 1968 encyclical in which he reaffirmed the Church's traditional teaching that any artificial interference with the human generative process, before, during, or following a marital act, is an intrinsically evil act — "birth control," in other words, is *wrong.*

This was the traditional teaching common to Christianity in its entirety for centuries — until the Church of England at its Lambeth Conference in 1929 conceded that "birth control" might be resorted to in "hard cases." From this single beginning on the part of one Christian communion, Christian opposition to the use of contraception was rather quickly abandoned nearly everywhere — except, of course, by the Catholic Church. Most people in our secularized society of today cannot even imagine any longer how there could be, or ever could have been, anything wrong with birth control; it seems such an immediate and obvious convenience and benefit. Thus, former Christendom is likely to be de-populated (or "Islamicized") before most people are ever likely to achieve even a glimmer of understanding concerning the insidious evil of contraceptive practice. Still, as the whole world still nevertheless knows, in his encyclical *Humanae Vitae*, Pope Paul VI unhesitatingly reiterated the Catholic Church's unchanging condemnation of it.

The question is: Are the Eastern Orthodox prepared to vindicate their claim that they alone have maintained and handed down unchanged the authentic Christian tradition in the case of what indisputably *was* the unanimous Christian tradition condemning the use of contraceptives? In the chapter which James Likoudis has devoted to this subject, he documents instances where the Orthodox too have justified recourse to the vice of contraception in marital relations, much as the Protestants have long since done with virtual unanimity — and just as prominent theological dissenters within the Catholic Church herself have attempted to do virtually since the encyclical *Humanae Vitae* was issued. However many modern Christians may dislike the thought, the fact is that recognizing the evil of contraception *is* a litmus test for traditional Christianity.

Thus, it should go without saying that this is yet *another* instance where the Orthodox have apparently *not* handed down, unchanged and intact, the traditional teaching and practice of Christ's Church. The controversies that have raged in the Church over the past generation should surely have made clear that: (1) the moral condemnation of birth control was indeed the *universal* teaching of *all* Christian Churches up to the time the Church of England broke ranks at Lambeth in 1929; and (2) since then the Catholic Church is the *only* remaining established Christian body that has maintained that venerable tradition intact. If the Orthodox way is the only true way, as the Orthodox still maintain, then they should have stood fast in defense of the traditional Christian teaching, just as the Catholic Church has. The fact that the Catholic Church has stood fast in the face of the contrary opinion of virtually the whole world surely provides yet another "motive of credibility" for the claims of her Magisterium.

James Likoudis further points out that the same kind of abandonment of traditional Christian teaching also applies to the Eastern Orthodox recognition of remarriage after divorce — another case where the Catholic Church, virtually alone, is found standing fast *contra mundum* (and in the face of opposition within her own ranks).

In raising these no doubt exceedingly unpopular and unwelcome teachings of the Church against birth control and remarriage after divorce, James Likoudis cannot help pointing to and thus raising yet another and prior question which has been too little considered or dealt with in ecumenical dialogue generally, namely, the question of what Christians in their various Churches and communion still actually continue to *believe* today, particularly on moral questions. The decline and, indeed, the near collapse of traditional sexual morality in modern society today has unfortunately to some extent been reflected in the current teaching and practice or practically every other Christian body except the Catholic Church — which alone, it would seem, has in fact, successfully, handed down the same moral teaching intact since apostolic times. And even though many individual Catholics apparently no longer accept the Church's teaching on certain disputed moral questions today, the fact remains that the Church's Magisterium has in no way changed. Nor can it change if the Church is really what she says she is.

These two books of James Likoudis are particularly valuable in understanding the Catholic-Orthodox situation across the whole range of outstanding issues. Virtually all of the major doctrinal, historical, and disciplinary issues which continue to stand in the way of reunion between the Catholic and Orthodox Churches are thoughtfully and accurately covered in these two volumes. Likoudis even gets into such questions as the influence of Orthodox theologian Gregory Palamas as an obstacle to mutual understanding.

He actually finds that there is an ontological relationship between the Trinitarian procession of the Holy Spirit from the Father and the Son, and the doctrine of the Petrine ministry of the bishop of Rome. Anyone who carefully reads and absorbs the content of these two books will be competent by that fact alone to engage in serious dialogue with the Eastern Orthodox. James Likoudis seems to hope for nothing more than that in all of his careful research and writing in these two books.

Of course it is true that conversions are not normally made merely by winning arguments. In the opinion of the present writer, however, the case made by Likoudis is pretty airtight and persuasive, even though the fact remains that not too many Orthodox are yet persuaded — along with a fair number of Catholics as well who simply eschew difficult "doctrinal" questions. Nevertheless, there is no substitute for honestly laying out the situation clearly as one sees it. Once the ecumenical situation becomes changed, as to some extent it already has been changed, by the sincere ecumenical outreach attempted by the popes and the Catholic Church since the Second Vatican Council, there is hope that the Eastern Orthodox too will become more susceptible to considering the kinds of facts and arguments laid out in these two volumes by James Likoudis.

At the same time there is no doubt that we Catholics can learn from the Orthodox as well. James Likoudis, in fact, shows evidence of having learned a great deal from them in the course of his long and arduous study of the Orthodox positions. It is therefore to be hoped that his efforts will help to contribute to the still hoped-for eventual reunion between the Catholic and Orthodox Churches.

CHAPTER NINETEEN

ROME'S *DOMINUS IESUS*

THE POST-CONCILIAR ROMAN pontiffs, like the Second Vatican Council itself, have consistently held that the new ecumenism adopted by Vatican II neither implied nor allowed for any doctrinal compromises on the part of the Catholic Church. It has always been strongly emphasized by Church authority that there could be no doctrinal minimalism or "splitting of differences" in order to achieve Christian unity. In spite of this, expectations were nevertheless created, in some minds at least, that in line with what was now perceived as the Church's obvious and sincere new commitment to ecumenism, she somehow *had* to have receded, or *would* recede, from what many thought were her once typical "extremist" claims to be the one, true — and visible — Church of Jesus Christ, the one, holy, Catholic, and apostolic Church of the Nicene Creed.

The many agreed statements produced by Church leaders and the various bilateral theological commissions perhaps helped to reinforce the idea in the minds of some that the Church would have had to recede from some of her previous claims if she were now truly committed to so many agreed statements as well as to ecumenism in general. How else could there be so many things that were suddenly "agreed upon" after all the disagreements, sometimes harsh and unbending and mutually condemnatory, that in some cases had endured for many centuries?

There was a fairly widespread popular assumption — nowhere strictly borne out in the actual documents agreed upon with non-Catholics in ecumenical dialogue, although some of these may have carefully remained silent on some topics — that, of course, the Catholic Church had to have backed off from, or at least to have moderated or muted somewhat, her former "intransigent" and even "extremist" claims. As a result, there erupted in the summer of the jubilee year 2000 something of a major crisis in ecumenical relations when the Congregation for the Doctrine of the Faith in Rome issued its Declaration *Dominus Iesus* on the Unicity and Salvific Universality of Jesus Christ and the Church. This CDF document, issued on August 6, 2000, immediately caused a furor, especially in ecumenical circles.

For in *Dominus Iesus,* in the minds of some, all of the supposedly moderated or abandoned maximalist claims of the Catholic Church appeared suddenly to have re-emerged. This was a misperception, since the idea that the Church had, or could have, abandoned any of her dogmatic claims, was the thing that was really mistaken. Nevertheless, this was the way many people viewed this Declaration from the Roman doctrinal Congregation. As the CDF Declaration explained it, the Second Vatican Council had sought "to harmonize two doctrinal statements: on the one hand, that the Church of Christ, despite the divisions which exist among Christians, continues to exist fully only in the Catholic Church; and on the other hand, that, outside her visible structure, many elements can be found of sanctification and truth" (DI 16).

But *Dominus Iesus* treated a number of other subjects as well. These subjects included: the definitiveness of the revelation of Jesus Christ; the Incarnate Logos and the Holy Spirit in the work of salvation; the unicity and universality of the mystery of Jesus; the unity or unicity of the Church; and the Church and other religions. The Catholic Church's traditional positions on these subjects were explicitly restated and reaffirmed. The document contained virtually *no* new Catholic doctrine, as a matter of fact; and, in fact, it was made up almost completely of quotations from previous Church documents, especially those issued or inspired by Vatican II. No one truly knowledgeable about what Catholic doctrine was should have been in any way surprised at what the document said; the surprise apparently arose from false expectations about what the Church's ecumenical commitment had meant.

The reason given for why the document was issued was that "in the practice of dialogue... new questions" had arisen, and the Congregation sought "to recall to bishops, theologians, and all the Catholic faithful *certain indispensable elements of Christian doctrine*" (DI 3; emphasis added). The fact that these "indispensable elements" of Christian doctrine were suddenly being recalled, reaffirmed, and insisted upon by the Congregation for the Doctrine of the Faith, however, suddenly seemed very offensive to some of the very people up to then engaged in dialogue. This was true even though the necessity for ecumenical dialogue was also reaffirmed in the CDF Declaration. It did not help that, when *Dominus Iesus* was released, the reporting about it tended to be greatly sensationalized. A story about it in the *Washington Post* (9/6/00), for example, was headlined: "Vatican Claims Church Monopoly on Salvation."

The impression created by this kind of reporting did not fail to cause disappointment, and even dismay, in some ecumenical circles. Nor were this disappointment and dismay allayed by the fact that the document was really not saying anything different from what the Catholic Church had been saying all along. The fact is that different expectations had arisen. Some Catholic as well as some non-Catholic theologians expressed disappointment with the document from the point of view of their particular perspectives. American Cardinals Francis George of Chicago, James Hickey of Washington, William Keeler of Baltimore, and Roger Mahony of Los Angeles all felt the need to issue public clarifying statements in order, apparently, to placate the critics of the document, as did more than a dozen other individual American archbishops and bishops. Even the past and current presidents of the Pontifical Council for Promoting Christian Unity, Australian Cardinal Edward Cassidy and German Cardinal

Walter Kasper, perhaps responding to or reflecting the concerns of their ecumenical "constituencies," appeared to distance themselves somewhat from the Declaration.

Dominus Iesus was greeted with particular disapproval by many Protestants. A Methodist theologian called the document "a jump backwards, a return to the past." Coinciding as it did with the celebrations for the beginning of the Third Millennium, the document was felt to have come at a particularly unhappy moment. The World Alliance of Reformed Churches considered canceling a planned dialogue in Rome following the release of the document (though, in the end, it did not do so). The Lutheran World Federation, which had just agreed to the Joint Declaration on Justification issued with the Catholic Church the year before, stated that "we are disappointed that 35 years of ecumenical dialogue between Roman Catholics and Lutherans seem not to have been considered in formulation of the letter and the documents issued by the Congregation for the Doctrine of the Faith."

The mention here of documents — plural — by the Lutheran World Federation also made reference to another document found to be unsatisfactory and controversial that had been issued by the Congregation on June 30, 2000. This latter document had been intended to be confidential within the Catholic Church. Nevertheless, it became public around the same time as *Dominus Iesus,* and served to feed the flames initially ignited by the latter. This second CDF document was a Doctrinal Note on "sister Churches." In it, the Congregation noted the revival of the term "sister Churches," a term originally employed in the East in antiquity to designate the patriarchal Churches of Rome, Antioch, Alexandria, Constantinople, and Jerusalem.

These patriarchal Churches that formed the ancient *Pentarchy,* as it was called, were commonly described as "sister Churches" in the East. No Roman pontiff, however, ever adopted this usage, which could imply that the pope in his then capacity as patriarch of the West was merely the head of another "sister Church" that was on the same level as the other four — that the pope, in other words, was simply the "first among equals," in accordance with the standard Eastern Orthodox viewpoint. The Eastern Orthodox were thus not happy when, in March, 2006, the Holy See dropped the use of the title the pope had borne for centuries (among his other titles) of "patriarch of the West." Although the pope truly had, and has, a special relationship with the Catholic Churches in the West, he is *more than just their patriarch*!

The CDF Doctrinal Note on the subject observed that the Ecumenical Patriarch Athenagoras I had first revived the term "sister Churches" in modern times when responding to fraternal gestures addressed to him by Blessed Pope John XXIII. Once the term had come back into use, though, it was picked up and employed in an informal way by both Paul VI and John Paul II in letters back and forth and the like (not in any teaching documents). The CDF Note was at pains to specify, however, that while the Church of Rome might in one sense indeed be styled the "sister Church" of another particular Church, such as the Church of Constantinople — or of the particular Churches of New York or Paris, for that matter — nevertheless, "one cannot properly say that the *Catholic Church* is the sister of a particular Church or group of Churches" (CDF Note 11; emphasis added). This is the case because "the one, holy, Catholic, and apostolic universal Church is not sister but *mother* of all the particular Churches" (CDF Note 10; emphasis in the original).

The CDF Note also re-enforced the long-held notion that some of the Christian communions with which the Catholic Church was officially in dialogue were not only *not* sister Churches; they were not Churches at all in the true sense of the word. *Dominus Iesus*, again, had stated this very plainly: "The ecclesial communities which have not preserved the valid episcopate and the genuine substance of the Eucharistic mystery are not Churches in the proper sense" (DI 17).

Vatican II had gotten around the problem created by this deficiency, of course, by referring to the Christian bodies lacking hierarchy or Eucharist as "ecclesial communities." Most of the Church's interlocutors in the ecumenical dialogue had long been aware of — and seemingly more or less accepting of — the distinction the Church intended to make by the use of this term. But when both *Dominus Iesus* and the CDF Doctrinal Note came out together in the Jubilee Year, not only reiterating the uniqueness of the Catholic Church, but, at the same time, pointedly reminding everyone of the non-Church status of some ecclesial communities, the result was not a little disillusioning for some of the Church's ecumenical partners. The Catholic Church's unwillingness in this document to obfuscate the issue of Church status proved to be a distinct irritant militating against continued smooth ecumenical relations once the issue was brought to the fore.

The Lutherans, in particular, took umbrage. The statement issued by the Lutheran World Federation said bluntly that there were Lutherans "not ready to accept the categories now emphasized by the Congregation for the Doctrine of the Faith." The statement recalled that in the Joint Declaration on Justification there was a clarifying note to the effect that "the word 'Church' is used in the Declaration 'to reflect the self-understanding of the particular Churches, without intending to resolve all the ecclesiological issues related to them.'" Presumably *Dominus Iesus* and the CDF Doctrinal Note should have availed themselves of the same method of avoiding the issue of Church status. Instead, however, the CDF had plainly "reverted," in the view of some dialogue partners, to the denial of the true status of a "Church" to some of those Christian bodies most committed to the ecumenical dialogue.

Such, then, was an example of the kind of unhappy outcome that could result from an ecumenical dialogue being too honestly carried on. No matter how often the Catholic Church might state that she could not give up any of her established doctrines in the interests of reaching ecumenical agreements, it was apparently widely assumed anyway that she could do so, and, in fact, necessarily would do so, or even had done so, by the very fact of entering into ecumenical dialogue at all. So when it became clear in *Dominus Iesus* and the CDF Doctrinal Note that the Church had *not* done so, the disillusionment was great, at least in some quarters. We have surely not heard the last of *Dominus Iesus*. There can be no question but that the honesty exhibited by this Declaration has had an effect, probably salutary in the long run, on the progress of ecumenism. The document, or something like it, was surely needed as a kind of reality check for ongoing ecumenical dialogues, and on all sides. The sheer lack of any serious controversy in some of these dialogues may have contributed to some of the false expectations that seem to have arisen and only became exposed after *Dominus Iesus* was issued.

However, it truly was a little short of amazing that the document aroused the furor that it did, considering the fact that there was nothing new in it; and that it was simply a reiteration of what the Catholic Church has always held and taught on the issues covered in it. Indeed, some might even have thought that it went too far the other way, at least in some respects. For example, as we have already mentioned in passing, the document actually reproduces the Nicene Creed just as it issued from the Councils of Nicaea and Constantinople, that is, *without* the *Filioque* clause! Many Eastern Orthodox writers, of course, have long accused the Catholic Church of having illegitimately added this clause, "and the Son," to what the ancient councils decreed. Catholics, of course, have rightly viewed the matter as a legitimate development of doctrine, which the Church has ably defended and justified for centuries. We have already taken note of the fact that the *Filioque* clause does not *have* to be in the Creed itself. On the other hand, there is something to be said for a vigorous defense of legitimate developments of doctrine such as this one.

Legitimate "developments of doctrine" (as of Church structures and institutions), it seems necessary to state once again, appear to constitute an issue which the Eastern Orthodox still, apparently, have to come to some serious terms with. Apparently, some Eastern Orthodox theologians have already agreed that the *Filioque* issue does not justify the separation between the Eastern and Western Churches, but it remains to be seen whether their Churches will ever officially agree to this.

Although there is nothing wrong or false about the wording of the Creed as it was formulated by the ancient Councils — Catholics *believe* what the ancient Councils decreed, after all! — simply leaving out, as *Dominus Iesus* does, this legitimate development of doctrine regarding the procession of the Holy Spirit, as it was authorized by the pope to be added to the Creed, is perhaps a case of "trying too hard" on the Catholic side. What we really need to do is to show and *convince* Orthodox Christians that the enactments and decisions taken in ecumenical Councils beyond the first seven recognized by them were both legitimate and necessary, as dictated by questions that arose at various times in history to which the Magisterium of Christ's *living* Church *had* to respond. Catholics continue to believe, after all, that all of these general Councils beyond the first seven recognized in both East and West still enjoyed the protection of the Holy Spirit against the teaching of any error.

Attempting to appease the Orthodox by simply acquiescing in their (short-sighted) view of, e.g., the *Filioque* issue, serves little purpose and it could be considered scandalous by some if the Catholic Church were seen to be repudiating the Creed she has recited for nearly a thousand years. There is nothing *wrong* with the *Filioque* clause, after all, and perhaps, therefore, it does need to be explained and defended.

In the end, there is no other basis except Christian truth on which Christian unity can be sought or concluded. This has been the consistent message both of Vatican II and of the post-conciliar popes. The Church has to be true to her own understanding of what she herself is (and, for example, what a "sister Church" is!). She cannot cut and trim for the sake of good ecumenical relations, and one of the things that *Dominus Iesus* has proven, once again, is that she *declines* to cut and trim for this purpose! Even as she honestly *cannot* grant true ecclesial status to all of her partners in the dialogue, however sincere *they* might be, she nevertheless does try to grant them their due. For *Dominus Iesus* repeats, in the very words of *Unitatis Redintegratio*, that:

> ... these separated Churches and communities as such, though we believe they suffer from defects, have by no means been deprived of significance and importance in the mystery of salvation. For the spirit of Christ has not refrained from using them as a means of salvation which derive their efficacy from the very fullness of grace and truth entrusted to the Catholic Church (UR 3).

What else besides this, given the claims that she makes, should the Catholic Church be obliged to concede? It is surely only on the basis of honesty that the ecumenical dialogue initiated at Vatican II can possibly proceed — in faith, certainly, but with honesty along with charity as well. How it all will all turn out is in any case in God's hands, as it has been all along.

CHAPTER TWENTY

THE NEW ECUMENISM CONFIRMED

I N HIS 2007 COMMENTARY on the Week of Prayer for Christian Unity, Pope Benedict XVI capped some remarks of his about the perceived slowness of the ecumenical process by noting that this process was "a journey which, after the initial difficulties, and even in their midst, also offers broad spaces of joy, refreshing stops, and from time to time allows one to breathe deeply the purest air of full communion." Pope Benedict then went on to say:

> The experience of recent decades after the Second Vatican Council demonstrates that the search for Christian unity takes place at various levels and in innumerable circumstances in parishes, in hospitals, in contacts between people, through the collaboration of local communities in every part of the world and, especially, in those regions where to make a gesture of good will for one's brother or sister demands a great effort and also a purification of memory.
>
> The meetings and events that constantly mark my ministry, the ministry of the Bishop of Rome, Pastor of the universal Church, also fit into this context of hope, punctuated by practical steps towards the full communion of Christians (*L'Osservatore Romano* - English Edition, January 31, 2007).

It seems clear from this statement of the pope that the Church's objective in her ecumenical outreach remains "the full communion of Christians." The Church has thus not been deflected from this aim by the lack of substantial progress towards reunion that has been achieved up to this point. The aim remains the same. The pope went on in his Commentary to pass in review the major ecumenical events in which he himself had participated personally in the course of the year 2006 — a not untypical year, in which one can see quite nicely where the new ecumenism now stands these forty plus years after *Unitatis Redintegratio* — and which we can reasonably expect also provides a kind of pattern for how things are likely to continue in the next few years.

In January, 2006, the pope received an official visit from representatives of the World Reformed Alliance in connection with a paper on "The Church as a Community of Common Witness to the Kingdom of God." This paper was then submitted for careful examination and the rendering of an ultimate judgment on it by the authorities of both the Catholic and the Reformed Churches. On January 25, 2006, the pope closed the annual Week of Prayer for Christian Unity with a ceremony in Rome's Basilica of St. Paul Outside the Walls which served as the solemn closing event of a meeting that had been convoked jointly by the European [Catholic] Episcopal Conferences and the Conference of [non-Catholic] European Churches. In May of 2006, the International Methodist-Catholic Dialogue Commission also completed its most recent report, entitled "The Grace Given You in Christ: Catholics and Methodists Reflect Further on the Church"; this report was then submitted to both Methodist and Catholic authorities.

Subsequently, the pope received at two of his weekly Wednesday Audiences delegations from both the Baptist World Alliance and the Evangelical Lutheran Church in America. Then there were the members of the hierarchy of the Orthodox Church of Georgia, who had come to pay their respects to the pope in Rome (it may be recalled that Georgia was one of the Orthodox countries where Pope

John Paul II had earlier received a rather mixed — if not actually hostile — reception).

Communications were also exchanged between the Churches on the occasion of the "Summit of Religious Leaders sponsored by the Russian Orthodox Church" which was held in Moscow in July, 2006. Patriarch Alexei II of Moscow, who had been so relatively unresponsive to the earlier suggestions by John Paul II regarding a possible visit by the latter to Russia, was now actually being characterized by Pope Benedict XVI as "having requested communion with the Holy See." What this actually meant or where it would lead was not completely clear; but following this, Metropolitan Kirill from the patriarchate of Moscow visited the pope in Rome in what Pope Benedict then characterized as "a more explicit normalization of our bilateral relations."

These steps, though perhaps small steps, nevertheless seemed to represent a marked advance in the relations between the Catholic Church and the Russian Orthodox Church — the largest, and the second largest, Christian Churches in the world, numerically speaking. Moreover, though contacts were increasing between the two Churches, there was still no indication of when further progress might be forthcoming. For example, in March, 2007, when a visit by President Vladimir Putin of Russia to Pope Benedict sparked rumors that Moscow Patriarch Alexei II would also be meeting with the pope, the Moscow patriarchate quickly issued a strong statement declaring such rumors to be "absolutely groundless."

In his year-end Commentary on the Week of Prayer for Christian Unity, Pope Benedict XVI also spoke favorably about the messages exchanged with the General Assembly of the World Council of Churches in Porto Alegre, Brazil, and with the General Assembly of the World Methodist Council in Seoul, Korea (at this latter meeting, the Methodists voted to sign and approve an official statement of association with the Joint Declaration on the Doctrine of Justification which the Catholic Church had concluded with the Lutheran World Federation in 1999).

In addition to these contacts, the pope received various delegations visiting Rome during 2006 such as Eastern Orthodox student groups and groups representing such organizations as "the Christian World Communions." While it may be asked what the ultimate point of such demonstrations of what would appear to be mere good fellowship might be, at least a partial answer to this — pertinent — question could be that such courtesy visits and exchanged messages at least make rather more difficult the continued characterization of the pope as a "tyrant," "usurper," or "heretic," etc. — as the pope was so regularly characterized not so long ago by some of the same groups and organizations that now respectfully seek to make contact and even conduct dialogue with him.

The pope then concluded his own summary of his ecumenical activities during 2006 with brief accounts of his meeting with the Anglican Archbishop of Canterbury in Rome, followed by his own visit to the Eastern Orthodox Ecumenical Patriarch in Istanbul later in the same month. After that, in December, 2006, the Greek Orthodox Archbishop of Athens and All Greece made an unprecedented visit to the pope in the Vatican. We can now look briefly at all three of these visits, which *do* provide a convenient "snapshot" look at where the new ecumenism generally stands these forty years and a little more after the end of the great Council which launched it.

Recent developments in the Anglican Communion, as we have already seen, have not exactly been auspicious as far as ecumenical relations with the Catholic Church are concerned. These relations had already been placed at risk awhile back with the first female ordinations in various Churches within the Anglican Communion. And we have already taken cognizance too of how the ordination of an openly practicing homosexual as a bishop by the Episcopal Church USA, like the permission of some Churches in the United States and Canada to allow blessings of homosexual unions, have now brought ceaseless turmoil into the Anglican Communion, not only in North America but worldwide. A number of Episcopal Churches in North America have announced their disaffiliation with the American Episcopalian body and have been seeking affiliation with African Churches within the Anglican Communion. The Episcopal Church USA, however, has declined to recognize these new affiliations. The primate of the Anglican Communion, Archbishop Rowan Williams of Canterbury, has struggled rather manfully to mediate this ongoing controversy, but he lacks the primatial authority to settle it.

This inconvenient fact is one which Catholics generally recognize as a serious, perhaps a fatal, defect in the Anglican, as in the Eastern Orthodox, systems: communions consisting of independent, "autocephalous," and perhaps "national" Churches, where the buck doesn't stop anywhere in cases like this, are simply *unable* to settle these kinds of differences within their own existing Church structures. No mechanism to mediate and settle such fundamental differences really exists. The Catholic system, resting on the primacy of the pope, has at various times in history been *unsuccessful* in settling such fundamental differences — obviously the schisms in Christianity exist and stem from these historic failures! But at least the *means* to settle such differences do exist within the Catholic system, and, very often, they have proved very successful in doing so.

Lacking such means, the leaders of the thirty-six Churches of the seventy-million-member Anglican Communion have met and deliberated and have passed resolutions insisting that the Episcopal Church USA must make a solemn commitment to abstain from and ban any further ordinations of persons living in willful defiance of Gospel moral standards. As of this writing, however, it does not seem likely that the Episcopal Church USA will agree to any such ecclesiastical requirement as a condition for continuing to maintain communion with the larger Anglican body. Further splintering and schism thus seem inevitable.

In any case, as far as ecumenical relations with the Catholic Church are concerned, the president of the Pontifical Council for Promoting Christian Unity, Cardinal Walter Kasper, had already, in June, 2006, in an address to the Church of England's House of

Bishops, warned the latter that Anglican-Catholic unity would be "out of reach" if the Anglican Communion continued with plans to ordain female bishops. Cardinal Kasper noted that "ecumenical dialogue in the true sense of the word has as its goal the restoration of full Church communion. That has been the presupposition of our dialogue until now. The presupposition would no longer exist following the ordination of women to the episcopal office." Yet in spite of Cardinal Kasper's sober words, about a month later, the Church of England synod adopted a statement saying that episcopal ordination of women was "consonant" with the faith of the Church of England (and, as it happens, the current presiding bishop of the Episcopal Church USA *is* a woman!).

This was the situation which obtained when Archbishop Rowan Williams visited Pope Benedict XVI in Rome on November 23, 2006. It must have weighed heavily upon the Anglican prelate. This was not the first visit of this archbishop of Canterbury with the pope, since he had previously met with Pope John Paul II in October of 2003. This 2006 visit, however, was thought to be particularly significant because it marked the fortieth anniversary of the day in 1964 when Pope Paul VI had welcomed Archbishop Michael Ramsey in the first meeting of a Roman pontiff with an archbishop of Canterbury since the Reformation more than four hundred years earlier. Yet in the 1960s, during Vatican Council II itself, hopes for Anglican-Catholic reunion had actually run quite high, but then the female ordination issue always had the potential to kill such hopes.

However that may be, this most recent meeting of the two bishops, of Rome and of Canterbury, judging by the discourse of each prelate on the occasion, as well as by the Common Declaration they issued, took place in an atmosphere of genuine, if not exquisite, mutual courtesy and respect. Both prelates made reference to the meeting of their predecessors in 1964 (but only Pope Benedict made reference to the fact that it was another one of *his* predecessors, Pope Gregory the Great, who had dispatched St. Augustine of Canterbury to fill that particular see some 1400 years earlier!).

It is surely quite understandable that, on this occasion, Archbishop Rowan would touch only very lightly on the circumstances that currently impeded, and most probably precluded, any further progress towards Anglican-Catholic reunion. He simply noted that "the path to unity is not an easy one, and that disputes about how we apply the Gospel to the challenges thrown up by modern society can often obscure or even threaten the achievements of dialogue, common witness, and service."

Pope Benedict, however, while specifically singling out for praise the substantial results of the theological dialogues that have been carried out between Anglicans and Catholics, nevertheless went on to remark, rather pertinently, that:

> Recent developments, especially concerning the ordained ministry and certain moral teachings, have affected not only internal relations with the Anglican Communion but also relations between the Anglican Communion and the Catholic Church.
>
> We believe that these matters, which are presently under discussion within the Anglican Communion, are of vital importance to the preaching of the Gospel in its integrity, and that your current discussions will shape the future of our relations.
>
> It is to be hoped that the work of the theological dialogue, which had registered no small degree of agreement on these and other important theological matters, will continue to be taken seriously in your discernment. In these deliberations, we accompany you with heartfelt prayer (*L'Osservatore Romano* - English Edition, November 29, 2006).

How could this have been put any better or with greater sensitivity? In their joint Common Declaration, the Roman pontiff and the Anglican primate specifically recognized the value of the work of both the Anglican-Roman Catholic International Commission (ARCIC), as well as that of the Anglican-Roman-Catholic Commission for Unity and Mission (IARCCUM). They then went on to declare that:

> In this fraternal visit, we celebrate the good which has come from these four decades of dialogue. We are grateful to God for the gifts of grace which have accompanied them.
>
> At the same time, our long journey together makes it necessary to acknowledge publicly the challenge represented by new developments which, besides being divisive for Anglicans, present serious obstacles to our ecumenical progress.
>
> It is a matter of urgency, therefore, that in renewing our commitment to pursue the path towards full, visible communion in the truth and love of Christ, we also commit ourselves to our continuing dialogue to address the important issues involved in the emerging ecclesiological and ethical factors making that journey more difficult and arduous (*L'Osservatore Romano* - English Edition, November 29, 2006).

Although one can surely grant the admirable consistency of the two prelates, and even the praiseworthy character of their "hoping against hope" (cf. Rom 4:18) in their continuing commitment to "pursue the path towards full, visible communion," it is hard not to conclude — with Cardinal Kasper — that in the present circumstances Anglican-Catholic unity is "out of reach." Barring some extraordinary new circumstances, the two communions will evidently continue in their separation, as has been the case for nearly 500 years.

As regards Pope Benedict XVI's visit to Ecumenical Patriarch Bartholomew I in Turkey, ecumenical hopes seemed much better grounded. The visit took place on November 30, 2006, the feast of St. Andrew the Apostle, the patron saint of Constantinople. But more was involved in this particular journey by the pope than just his visit to the patriarch. The pope was also visiting a Muslim country, Turkey, in the wake of what had become a worldwide controversy which had been stirred up by an academic address which Benedict had delivered at the University of Regensburg, in his native Germany, in September, 2006. In his Regensburg address, the pope had quoted the rather harsh words of a fourteenth-century Byzantine emperor concerning the Prophet Mohammed which many Muslims had interpreted both as an attack on their prophet and on the reasonableness of their faith. Much anti-Benedict sentiment among Muslims was thus manifested around the world. Pope Benedict was in any case controversial in Turkey because of views which he had expressed earlier as a cardinal opposing the admittance of Turkey into the European Union (by the time the pope arrived in Turkey, however, this latter position seemed to have become modified as a result of further statements emanating from the Vatican).

In the event, the Turkish and Muslim aspects of the pope's visit seem to have been something of an almost unalloyed triumph for him. He met with the President of the Turkish Republic, the Prime Minister, and the President for Religious Affairs. He visited the Mausoleum of Mustafa Kemal Atatürk, founder of the Turkish Republic, as well as Istanbul's famous Blue Mosque, where it was reported in the world press and media that the pope had bowed his head and moved his lips in prayer. He himself wrote later that he had "addressed the One Lord of heaven and earth, the Merciful Father of all humanity"; and he added: "May all believers recognize that they are his creatures and witness to true brotherhood"!

However, the pope's visit *was* intended to be primarily a religious one, and hence, in addition to his visit to Bartholomew I, he also went to the site of ancient Ephesus, where he celebrated Mass at the shrine of Mary's House, which the Apostle John had had built for the Mother of God not far from where the Council of Ephesus in 431 had proclaimed her to be *Theotokos*, or God-bearer.

The meeting with Bartholomew I was the latest in what had become a fairly regular series of visits exchanged between pope and patriarch. Like Pope John Paul II before him, Pope Benedict XVI treated this meeting with the utmost seriousness as a major event in the life of the Church. In some ways, this may seem anomalous, considering that the Church of Constantinople finds itself today in a country that is more than 99 percent Muslim, boasts active members only in the low thousands, occupies little more than a "compound" of its own in Istanbul, and operates under other severe restrictions imposed by the secular Turkish state. For example, the patriarchate is not even allowed to have its own seminary. Turkish authorities actually claim that if they allowed a Christian Church to sponsor its own school, they would have to allow such religious schools, currently banned, for extremist Muslim groups as well!

Historically, however, the city of Constantinople was the capital of the Byzantine Empire and was the "New Rome." Its patriarch is still recognized by the fourteen or so national autocephalous Eastern Orthodox Churches as the "first among equals." This does not mean, however, that he occupies a position within the Eastern Orthodox communion comparable to that of the pope within the Catholic communion. He could not, for example, ever conclude any kind of agreement with the pope that would then apply in the Orthodox Churches in communion with him. Any agreements between the Catholic Church and the Eastern Orthodox Churches would have to be approved by each of them. It thus seems clear that the respect paid to the patriarch is largely symbolical (but it demonstrates, it would seem, that the Catholic Church *does* respect Orthodox traditions!).

Thus, the popes have continued to consider relations with the patriarch of Constantinople to be very important. Nor, as a matter of fact, is it easy to see how the Catholic-Orthodox dialogue could go forward without him. Bartholomew I was essential, it was reported, in getting fourteen national Orthodox Churches to participate in the renewed dialogue being conducted by the Joint International Commission for Theological Dialogue between the Orthodox Church and the Catholic Church, which had resumed its work at a meeting in Belgrade in September, 2006, after a hiatus of more than five years.

The actual encounter between the pope and the patriarch took place at the Patriarchal Church of St. George at the Phanar in Istanbul on the feast of St. Andrew the Apostle, November 30, 2006. Also present was the Armenian Orthodox Patriarch Mesrob II, whom the pope had joined at his cathedral in Istanbul for a joint prayer service. At this meeting in the Phanar, the pope attended a Divine Liturgy celebrated by the Ecumenical Patriarch Bartholomew I, where the latter also preached; and then the pope contributed an address of his own. Following this Divine Liturgy, the two prelates jointly blessed the faithful gathered in the courtyard in both Latin and Greek. They then repaired to the Phanar Throne Room where their Joint Declaration was read and signed.

Bartholomew I, in his homily, spoke mainly on the subject of the liturgy itself, which he described as "a powerful and spiritual celebration, joining heaven and history." He alluded only briefly and with reticence to the ecumenical question when he noted that "with deep sorrow we confess that we cannot yet celebrate the Holy Mysteries together and may that the day will come on which this sacramental unity will be fully expressed."

Benedict XVI dwelt at perhaps surprising length on Andrew, Simon Peter's brother, the patron saint of the Church of Constantinople. While Andrew was perhaps not historically the actual "founder" of the Church at Byzantium with which tradition credits him, he has nevertheless for centuries been considered the patron of the bishops of Constantinople, and it does not in the least seem inappropriate that he should continue to be so considered. Benedict XVI evidently chose to emphasize this connection with conscious deliberation out of respect for the Byzantine tradition. He stressed the fact that Peter and Andrew *were* brothers, and that, indeed, it was Andrew who first brought his brother Simon to Jesus (cf. Jn 1:40 ff.). At the same time, the pope quite understandably reminded everyone again of what John Paul II had called the "Petrine service of unity." "The issue of the universal service of Peter and his successors has unfortunately given rise to our differences of opinion," the pope emphasized. He added that "we hope to overcome [these differences] thanks also to the theological dialogue which has been recently resumed."

In their Joint Common Declaration, the fourth in the series concluded between Rome and Constantinople — beginning with the one Pope John Paul II issued in conjunction with Ecumenical Patriarch Dimitrios I on November 30, 1979 — both Churchmen declared that "the Holy Spirit will help us to prepare the great day of re-establishment of full unity, whenever and however God wills it." They recalled the legacy of their predecessors, who had called for dialogue in charity. They covered a number of areas of joint concern such as the preservation of the Christian roots of Europe, respect for the rights of all human beings, peace in the Middle East, protection of the natural environment, and the impact of a culture of "economic and technological progress that does not know its limits." Above all, however, the pope and the patriarch declared that:

> As pastors, we have first of all reflected on the mission to proclaim the Gospel in today's world. This mission, "Go make disciples of all nations" (Mt:28-19), is today more timely and necessary than ever in traditionally Christian countries. Moreover, we cannot ignore the increase of secularization, relativism, even nihilism, especially in the Western world. All this calls for a renewed and powerful proclamation of the Gospel, adapted to the cultures of our times. Our traditions represent for us a patrimony that must be continually shared, proposed, and interpreted anew. This why we must strengthen our cooperation and our common witness before the world (*L'Osservatore Romano* - English Edition, December 8, 2006).

And just as Pope Benedict saw fit to visit Patriarch Bartholomew on the feast of St. Andrew at the end of 2007, so the latter reciprocated by coming to Rome again in person for the celebrations of the feast of Saints Peter and Paul on June 29, 2008 — where the two prelates, among other things, recited the Nicene Creed in Greek together *without* the *Filioque* clause!

All in all, then, the state of the official relations between the Catholic and Eastern Orthodox communions has to be viewed in a rather favorable light. There has been real, tangible ecumenical progress in spite of difficulties and setbacks which have impeded this progress to some extent (and no doubt will continue to do so in ways not now foreseeable). Both sides continue to speak optimistically about further possible progress, however, and where there is a will there can also be a way. By itself the progress that has already been made in the relations between East and West, along with the promise of more to come, would seem to provide by itself ample justification for the adventure of the new ecumenism embarked on so hopefully more than forty years earlier.

Moreover, this tangible progress on the Orthodox front received added, and, indeed, rather dramatic, new impetus just two weeks after Benedict XVI's meeting with Bartholomew I. What happened was that Archbishop Christodoulos of Athens and All Greece came to visit the pope in Rome. It was a return visit, long planned to follow up on the visit Pope John Paul II had made to Athens in 2001. That earlier visit had been one during which it was not entirely clear from the published reports that the Polish pope's Greek hosts had the same enthusiasm for the visit of a Roman pontiff that John Paul himself had. In fact, back then, Athens was still considered to be one of the places in the Orthodox world least open to the new ecumenism. Archbishop Christodoulos did receive John Paul II at that time — it was in May, 2001 — and they did issue the usual Joint Common Statement. This particular statement, however, did not venture far into ecclesiastical questions, but mostly focused on the evils of war, terrorism, and violence, and the desirability of peace; on globalization; and on hopes for the success of the European Union. It was on the occasion of this 2001 visit to Greece, by the way, that Pope John Paul II had tendered one of his famous "apologies," in this case an apology for the sack of Constantinople by Western knights in the year 1204.

The Common Declaration of December 14, 2006, between

Archbishop Christodoulos and Pope Benedict XVI, however, starts right off by declaring that "our meeting in *charity* makes us ever more conscious of our common task: to travel together along the arduous route of a *dialogue in truth* with a view to establishing the full communion of faith in a bond of love" (emphasis in the original). The two prelates then re-committed their respective Churches to the quest for Christian unity in even stronger terms, as follows:

> We unanimously declare the need to persevere on the path of constructive theological dialogue. Despite the difficulties noted, this path is one of the essential means we have at our disposal to re-establish around the altar of the Lord the unity so longed for by the Ecclesial Body, and likewise to strengthen the credibility of the Christian message in this period of social upheaval in which we live, amid the great spiritual hunger of so many of our contemporaries who are anxious about the increasing globalization that sometimes even threatens man's existence and his relationship to God and to the world.
>
> In a very special way, we solemnly renew our desire to proclaim the Gospel of Jesus Christ to the world, especially to the new generation, because "the love of Christ impels us" (II Cor 5:14) (*L'Osservatore Romano* - English Edition, January 3, 2007).

In the course of his visit to Rome, Archbishop Christodoulos was presented with a reliquary containing two links from the chain that had once bound St. Paul himself in prison, prior to his beheading. These chain links had been preserved since ancient times and venerated in the Roman Basilica of St. Paul Outside the Walls — a Church that was built over St. Paul's tomb. To be able to part with a relic as precious as this surely constitutes one more demonstration of the Holy See's faith and hope in the eventual reunion of Catholics with the Eastern Orthodox.

CHAPTER TWENTY-ONE

PROSPECTS FOR THE FUTURE

T HE NEW ECUMENISM has wrought many changes in the Church's life since it got launched following the mandate of the Second Vatican Council. The open, regular, and even frequent contacts that are common among Christian leaders today were unheard and even unimaginable before Vatican II. Nor are these friendly contacts and relationships limited to Christian leaders. Christians in the pews in various Churches and denominations generally also tend to be more friendly today and to interact more readily with each other than was formerly the case. This is especially, though not exclusively the case with what has come to be called "the ecumenism of the trenches" — the cooperation between Christians of various confessions in opposing some of the grave evils stemming from the galloping moral degradation in our society today, evils such as abortion, assisted suicide, biotechnological and embryonic experimentation and exploitation, so-called emergency contraception, euthanasia, marriage and family break ups, widespread cohabitation outside marriage, epidemic single parenthood, and the moral acceptance of homosexual relations and so-called "same-sex marriage."

Of course there is no moral unanimity even among Christians on these and other moral issues in what Pope John Paul II so aptly called today's "culture of death" — and Benedict XVI, with equal aptness, called today's "dictatorship of relativism." Yet in spite of the unprecedented challenges of some of the moral issues that confront us with immediacy today — and in spite of the gravity and seriousness with which the Church's Magisterium has tried to face up to these same typically modern evils — many Christians, and among them many Catholics, often show little or no concern at all over the "culture wars" that have been going on over these issues for some time now in our society.

Worse, it seems obvious that some of our fellow Christians, again with a fair number of Catholics among them, have even "joined the other side" in these culture wars. We need think in this connection only of the ill-starred efforts of some American Catholic bishops at the time of the 2004 elections in America to try to make clear to Catholic politicians and other public figures who openly support evils such as legalized abortion that they are guilty of formal cooperation with evil and hence should not present themselves for Holy Communion. These efforts were initially encouraged by none other than Cardinal Joseph Ratzinger himself, but it turned out that few American bishops were prepared to press the issue, especially since the indifference and even sometimes the opposition of their own faithful appeared to be massive. The whole affair proved to be one more case where the Church had to draw back rather ignominiously in the face of the triumphant and unapologetic aggressiveness of the dominant secular culture.

It is true that Catholics can be consoled to some degree by the realization that at least the Church's Magisterium has not failed us in consistently and correctly identifying and labeling these contemporary evils for what they are, even if in practice the Church's teachings are not more widely accepted and acted upon, even by many of the Church's own faithful. Nevertheless, the lack of even any minimal Christian consensus on the grave moral issues of our day — not to speak of unanimity! — is not the least serious casualty of the continuing lack of Christian unity.

Even so, it would seem on balance that Christian witness to the world, to the extent that it remains effective at all, has been enhanced as a result of the new ecumenism. Christ's commandment to his followers to "love one another as I have loved you" (Jn 15:12), to the degree to which it is actually followed, has always been the best advertisement for Christianity. Christianity in general is obviously more credible if Christians are *not* fighting with each other, and this is the case even if they are not otherwise too effective, as is unhappily often the case today, in defending Christianity itself.

Still, the sobering fact that remains, forty plus years after the launching of the new ecumenism, at the very time when the world needs a fruitful Christian witness more than ever, there are scarcely any real and tangible instances of actual Christian reunion. Christian reunion was, and remains, the declared aim of the new ecumenism. There has been much progress in developing better relations among Christians, as we have seen, but even after all the positive dialogue, the mutual compliments exchanged, the visits back and forth, the agreed statements, and even charitable work in common, hardly anybody yet seems ready to ask, much less answer, the blunt question: "Why not reunion now?" Most certainly, almost nobody outside the Catholic Church has shown any signs of willingness at all to accept what would necessarily have to be the Catholic Church's conditions for any true reunion.

On the contrary, typical public statements by Church leaders on all sides, including sometimes the Catholic side, seem to take for granted that the ecumenical road before us remains long and hard and its terminus is not only nowhere in sight but in fact seems constantly to recede like a mirage before us with each successful ecumenical achievement or agreement. This is actually the case even with Pope Benedict XVI himself, than whom nobody is more committed to the necessity for the ecumenical journey. But as we saw in his Commentary on the Week of Prayer for Christian Unity in 2007, he sees ecumenism as "a slow process, sometimes even discouraging.... It is a slow and uphill journey like every penitential process" (*L'Osservatore Romano* - English Edition, January 31, 2007).

However, what should not be imagined, even for a moment,

is that there has been any weakening of resolve on the part of the Catholic Church in the pontificate of Benedict XVI to carry on with the Church's commitment to move ahead with the ecumenical process in spite of the setbacks that have been encountered (such as the decision of the Church of England to proceed with female ordination, contrary to the practice of Christ) — and in spite of perhaps inevitable discouragement and lack of tangible results as well. We should be reminded that Pope Benedict actually prefaced the remarks we have just quoted on the slowness and difficulties of the ecumenical process by going back to the original commitment made by Vatican II:

> The concern for restoring unity involves the whole Church, faithful and clergy alike. It extends to everyone, according to the talent of each, whether it be exercised in daily Christian living or in theological and historical studies (Decree on Ecumenism, *Unitatis Redintegratio*, 5).

These and similar remarks have been re-iterated frequently by the popes, and nearly always in the same vein. There can be no question concerning the Catholic Church's continuing commitment to the on-going ecumenical process. As Pope John Paul II stated in *Ut Unum Sint*: "At the Second Vatican Council the Catholic Church committed herself *irrevocably* to following the path of the ecumenical venture" (UUS 3; italics in the original). *Aficionados* of Church history know that the Catholic Church does not abandon or reverse herself on positions adopted at this level with this kind of seriousness. Even if reunion is not achieved (or is not achieved *soon*), other benefits accrue simply as a result of participation in the process.

Thus, if we ask ourselves whether Vatican II's decision to adopt a policy of active ecumenical involvement for the Catholic Church was, let us say, a providential turn, or, rather instead, a historic mistake, I believe we have to opt for the former and reject the latter. Blessed Pope John XXIII was basically right. The quest for Christian unity in his day was at a standstill and this was intolerable, a true scandal. Christ's prayer "that they may all be one" was being steadily disregarded on all sides, and, indeed, in certain ways, was virtually *forgotten*. How could Christians disregard, or, worse, forget, a prayer of Christ himself in this way?

And if we ask what Christian body should have taken the lead in trying to provide a remedy for this unhappy situation, we cannot neglect or ignore the idea that it should have been the Christian body which continues to claim the fullness of Christ's truth and grace, namely, the Catholic Church. The decision of the Fathers of Vatican Council II to adopt the new ecumenism was thus altogether fitting and proper. Catholics should accordingly embrace the new ecumenism, just as all the popes since Vatican II quite manifestly have adopted it, indeed, have embraced it.

No doubt the continuing lack of tangible results, after so much effort, in the form of any actual Christian reunification anywhere, continues to disappoint. Yet even though the course adopted at Vatican II was basically the correct one, perhaps the expectations of any quick or early success were exaggerated, especially considering the long separations. It was none other than Cardinal Joseph Ratzinger, the future Pope Benedict XVI, who, nearly twenty years ago, warned us in his book *Church, Ecumenism, and Politics*, of the necessity of recognizing:

> ... the limits of what one might term the "ecumenism of negotiation" and not to expect of it any more than it can provide: rapprochements in important human fields, but not unity itself. It seems to be that many disappointments could have been avoided if this had been clear from the start. But after the successes of the early period just after the Council, many have understood ecumenism as a diplomatic task in political categories; [and] just as one expects of good negotiators that after some time they will

come to a joint agreement that is acceptable to everyone, so people thought they could expect this of the Church authorities in matters of ecumenism. But this was to expect too much of the ecumenical movement....

More recently, the man who became Pope Benedict XVI, in his book entitled *Pilgrim Fellowship of Faith: The Church as Communion*, reminded us even more pertinently that:

> We had, in fact, overrated our capacities if we believed that theological dialogues could, within a fairly brief time span, restore the unity of belief. We had lost our way if we got it into our heads that this goal must be reachable within deadlines we had laid down. For a little while we were confusing theology with politics, confusing dialogues with belief about diplomacy. We wanted to do ourselves what only God can do. That is why we have to be prepared to keep on seeking, in the knowledge that the seeking itself is one way of finding: that being on a journey and traveling on, without stopping to take rest, is the only appropriate attitude for the person who is on a pilgrimage toward eternity.

In early 2008, the Archbishop of Cracow, Cardinal Stanislaw Dziwisz, who had been the private secretary of Pope John Paul II, published a memoir entitled *A Life with Karol: My Forty Year Friendship with the Man Who Became Pope*. To conclude this book, it seems fitting to quote something of what Cardinal Dziwisz records about Pope John Paul II's attitude towards the new ecumenism. In a chapter entitled "It Took Six Hands," the Polish cardinal (and successor to Karol Wojtyla himself in the See of Cracow) writes:

> John Paul II was pushing manfully, but he just couldn't seem to get the Holy Door to open. For on-lookers at St. Paul Outside the Walls who didn't know what was go-

ing on, there was a moment of embarrassment. Only a moment, though. Because it immediately became clear: It wasn't that the Pope couldn't open the door but that he was waiting. He was waiting for the Orthodox Metropolitan Athanasios and the Archbishop of Canterbury George Carey to lend a hand. With all six hands pushing, the door swung open. And then all three knelt in unison.

For the first time in history, the Bishop of Rome, the Successor of Peter and the most senior representatives of Orthodox and Protestantism jointly opened a Holy Door and stepped side by side into the Basilica of the Apostle of the Gentiles, which as such is the ecumenical basilica par excellence...

The scene we've just described, which took place on January 19, 2000, symbolized the whole trajectory of the ecumenical movement, with all its peaks and valleys....

...in order to re-establish friendly and brotherly relations with the different Orthodox Churches, John Paul II undertook, with some risk a series of trips to places like Romania, where the issue of the Eastern Catholic Church was still unresolved, Greece, where the Orthodox bishops hadn't even invited him to come; Moscow's neighbor, Ukraine. And yet he was aided by his *mea culpas* and buoyed up by the conviction that, as he would often put it, the first step was to promote "union in feeling and then union in deed." As a result, the Pope was able to effect a radical change in places and in attitudes that were hostile before.

I'm still moved when I remember how, during the Holy Father's visit to Bucharest, the people suddenly burst out shouting, *"Unitade, unitade"* ("Unity, unity"). Everybody joined in — Orthodox, Catholics, Evangelical Protestants. All of them were shouting for the unity that once existed among Christians.

I'd also like to mention... his visit to Greece because it was a really extraordinary event. During the Holy Father's stay in Athens, we saw two Churches overcome their initial distance and draw closer together by the hour. By the time the Pope left, the Greek Orthodox Church was no longer the same as it was when he had arrived in Greece.

Well, then, how long will we have to wait for the reunion of all Christians? This is a question that even Pope John Paul II asked himself at the end of *Ut Unum Sint*: "*Quanta est nobis via*"? How much further do we still have to go? Maybe the six hands that together pushed open the ancient Byzantine door of St. Paul's were themselves already a first answer. For those hands belonged to Christians who, while still divided, truly wished to come back together again some day.

SELECTED BIBLIOGRAPHY

Broderick, John F., S.J., *Documents of Vatican Council I* (1869-1870), The Liturgical Press, Collegeville, MN, 1971.

Bunson, Matthew E., General Editor, 2007 *Catholic Almanac*, Huntington, IN: Our Sunday Visitor Publishing Division, 2007.

Cassidy, Cardinal Edward Idris, *Ecumenism and Interreligious Dialogue: Unitatis Redintegratio, Nostra Aetate*, New York/Mahwah, NJ: Paulist Press, 2005.

Clément. Olivier, *You Are Peter: An Orthodox Theologian's Reflection on the Exercise of the Papal Primacy*, New York: New City Press, 2003.

Congregation for the Doctrine of the Faith, Declaration on the Unicity and Salvific Universality of Jesus Christ and the Church, *Dominus Iesus*. August 6, 2000 (In *Origins: CNS Documentary Service*, September 14, 2000, Vol. 30; No. 14).

Congregation for the Doctrine of the Faith, Note on the Expression "Sister Churches," June 30, 2000 (In *Origins: CNS Documentary Service*, September 14, 2000, Vol. 30; No. 14).

Congregation for the Doctrine of the Faith, Reflections on the Primacy of the Successor of Peter in the Mystery of the Church, October 30, 1998 (In *L'Osservatore Romano* - English Edition, November 18, 1998).

Congregation for the Doctrine of the Faith, Letter to the Bishops of the Catholic Church on Some Aspects of the Church Understood As Communion, *Communionis Notio*, May 28, 1992, Boston: St. Paul Books and Media, 1992.

Dziwisz, Cardinal Stanislaw, *A Life with Karol: My Forty Year Friendship with the Man Who Became Pope*. In conversation with Gian Franco Svidercoschi. New York: Doubleday, 2008.

Fesquet, Henri, *The Drama of Vatican II: The Ecumenical Council-June, 1962 - December, 1965*, New York: Random House, 1967.

Flannery, Austin, O.P., Editor, *Vatican Council II: The Conciliar and Post-Conciliar Documents*, Northport, NY: Costello Publishing Co., 1977.

Flannery, Austin, O.P., Editor, *Vatican Council II: More Postconciliar Documents*, Northport, NY: Costello Publishing Co., 1982.

Garuti, Rev. Adriano, O.F.M., *Primacy of the Bishop of Rome and the Ecumenical Dialogue*, San Francisco: Ignatius Press, 2004.

Hebblethwaite, Peter, *Pope John XXIII: Shepherd of the Modern World*, New York: Doubleday, 1985.

Hebblethwaite, Peter, *Paul VI: The First Modern Pope*, New York/Mahwah, NJ: Paulist Press, 1993.

John Paul II, Pope, Encyclical Letter on Commitment to Ecumenism, *Ut Unum Sint* ["That They May All Be One,"], dated May 25, 1995, Boston: Pauline Books and Media, 1995.

John Paul II, Pope, Encyclical Letter on the Redeemer of Man, *Redemptor Hominis*, dated March 4, 1979, Washington, DC: U.S. Catholic Conference Publications Office, 1979.

Kasper, Cardinal Walter, Editor, *The Petrine Ministry: Catholics and Orthodox in Dialogue*, New York/Mahwah, NJ: Paulist Press, 2006.

Kasper, Walter, *That They All May Be One: The Call to Unity Today*, London: Burns & Oates, 2004.

Likoudis, James, *The Divine Primacy of the Bishop of Rome and Modern Eastern Orthodoxy: Letters to a Greek Orthodox on the Unity of the Church*, P.O. Box 852, Montour Falls, NY 14865, 2002.

Likoudis, James, *Eastern Orthodoxy and the See of Peter,* P.O. Box 852, Montour Falls, NY 14856, 2006.

Meyendorff, John, Editor, *The Primacy of Peter: Essays in Ecclesiology and the Early Church*, Crestwood, NY: St. Vladimir's Seminary Press, 1992.

Paul VI, Pope, Encyclical Letter on the Paths of the Church, *Ecclesiam Suam*, Boston: St. Paul Editions, 1964.

Ratzinger, Cardinal Joseph (Pope Benedict XVI), *Church, Ecumenism, & Politics: New Essays in Ecclesiology*, New York: Crossroad Books, 1987.

Ratzinger, Cardinal Joseph (Pope Benedict XVI), *Pilgrim Fellowship of Faith: The Church As Communion*, San Francisco: Ignatius Press, 2005.

Ratzinger, Cardinal Joseph (Pope Benedict XVI), *Called to Communion: Understanding the Church Today*, San Francisco: Ignatius Press, 1991.

Stacpoole, Alberic, O.S.B., Editor, *Vatican II Revisited: By Those Who Were There*, Minneapolis: Winston Press, 1986.

Weigel, George, *Witness to Hope: The Biography of Pope John Paul II*, New York: HarperCollins, 1999.

Wiltgen, Ralph M., S.V.D., *The Rhine Flows into the Tiber: The Unknown Council*, New York: Hawthorn Books, 1967.

ABOUT THE AUTHOR

Kenneth D. Whitehead is a former Assistant Secretary of Education appointed by President Ronald Reagan. Prior to that, among other positions, he was a career Foreign Service Officer for some ten years stationed in American embassies in Rome, the Middle East, and North Africa. For eight years he was Executive Vice President of Catholics United for the Faith. Since retiring, he works as a writer, lecturer, editor, and translator in Falls Church, Virginia. He is the author of hundreds of articles, and of some eight books, most recently, *One, Holy, Catholic, and Apostolic: The Early Church Was the Catholic Church* (Ignatius Press, 2000). With James Likoudis, he is the co-author of *The Pope, the Council, and the Mass* (25th Anniversary Revised Edition: Emmaus Road Publishing, 2006), a study of the "changes" in the liturgy following the Second Vatican Council. Earlier he co-authored (with Monsignor Michael J. Wrenn) *Flawed Expectations: The Reception of the Catechism of the Catholic Church* (Ignatius Press, 1996). He has translated more than twenty books from French, German, or Italian, and he is the editor of some half dozen other books, most recently, *The Church, Marriage, and the Family* (St. Augustine's Press, 2007). Mr. Whitehead was educated at the University of Utah and the University of Paris, and he holds an honorary degree as a Doctor of Christian Letters from the Franciscan University of Steubenville. Mr. Whitehead is married to the former Margaret O'Donohue, a professional religious educator, and they are the parents of four grown sons.

INDEX